JESUS
f✡r Jews

Stories of Jews Who Believe in Jesus

JESUS
f✡r Jews

Stories of Jews Who Believe in Jesus

PURPLE POMEGRANATE PRODUCTIONS

Jesus for Jews
edited by Susan Perlman, Ruth Rosen and Naomi Rose Rothstein
© Copyright 2006 by Purple Pomegranate Productions
(a division of Jews for Jesus®)
Cover design by David Yapp

For more information, including reprint permission, write to:
Jews for Jesus®
60 Haight Street
San Francisco, CA 94102
USA
www.jewsforjesus.org

ISBN 10: 1 881022 65 X
ISBN 13: 978 1 881022 65 7

Contents

Introduction

Why don't Jews believe in Jesus? This is a question that perplexes many Christians. It seems to them that if anyone ought to believe in Jesus, it should be Jewish people. After all, Jesus was a Jew and it was to the Jewish people that he made himself known.

Most Jewish people have a variety of reasons to explain why they don't believe in Jesus. Yet, as one listens to the many reasons given, two things become apparent. First, most Jewish people have never really, seriously contemplated whether or not Jesus might possibly be the Messiah. It is simply not an open question. And second, there seems to be a commitment to believe that he is NOT the Messiah. The reasons commonly given for the commitment to unbelief often sound like afterthoughts— justifications for a decision already made. That is because so many Jewish people see the commitment not to believe in Jesus as necessary to our survival.

In other words, to believe in Jesus is seen as contradictory to caring about one's Jewish identity, as if being Jewish and believing in Jesus are antithetical to one another. We Jews know who and what we are; we know our own history and what our people have endured. We have plenty of good reasons for rejecting Christian beliefs (at least those reasons seem good to us).

Many Jewish people find it difficult to admit it's the rejection of Christians and not Jesus himself that keeps us from believing. But who is it that is blamed for the Holocaust? The Pogroms? The Crusades?

The fact that Jesus spoke against violence and against the persecution of any and all people should demonstrate that the perpetrators of such atrocities were not acting "Christianly." They were using religion to justify or excuse their blatantly unchristian conduct.

The commitment to Jewishness involves survival instincts which include the attraction of "our own" and the rejection and exclusion of those who are "not our own."

Buried beneath some rather esoteric theological reasons for not believing in Jesus is the pivotal fact: Jews don't believe in Jesus simply because we want to be Jews and we have been indoctrinated that the religion of Jesus belongs to "them" not to "us."

It was not so in the beginning. The last in the lineage of Jewish prophets, Yochanan (John), had a message of repentance to bring to Israel. Large crowds gathered as this prophet pointed to Jesus and called him "the Lamb of God."[1] Two of John's followers determined to investigate the matter. After interviewing Jesus, they went out to tell others. Philip put it succinctly when he said, "We have found Him of whom Moses in the law and also the prophets wrote."[2] This testimony of discovery was how knowledge of and faith in Jesus were spread: from one Jewish person to another. Some were convinced by the miracles, others by his wisdom and, to some, there were direct revelations from God himself.

A seemingly chance encounter Jesus had with a Samaritan woman had her running to tell the people of her city, "Come, see a man who told me all things that I ever did. Could this be the Messiah?"[3] After hearing her report, they came, they saw, they listened and they told her, "Now we believe, not because of what you said, for we ourselves have heard him and we know that this is indeed the Messiah . . ."[4]

That is the invitation of this book.

If you already know Jesus and believe in him, your story will resonate with the four in this book. If you don't yet believe, listen to what these people have to say, what they've discovered, and investigate for yourself the evidence that, indeed, Jesus is the promised One for all people. He is not "for Gentiles only." *Jesus is for Jews.*

Endnotes
1. John 1:29
2. John 1:45
3. John 4:29
4. John 4:42

Nothing to Fear

By Karol Joseph

I emerged from the subway hole into the crowded streets of New York City, terrified. I looked around Times Square and saw pimps, prostitutes and drug addicts. I said aloud, "Now this could be dangerous." I wanted to disappear. But that was nothing new. I had been afraid for most of my life.

My name is Karol Beth Joseph. I was born in Boston,
Massachusetts on August 16, 1952, the third of four
children born to my mother, Renee, and my father,
Alvin—both Jewish. My father is a certified public
accountant. My mother—a Brooklynite who moved to
Boston to marry my father—made a career of raising us
kids and was a very active volunteer with organizations
like the ORT (Occupational and Rehabilitation Training).

I grew up in Newton, Massachusetts (about eight miles
from Boston) in a community so Jewish I only knew one
Gentile girl in my whole elementary school. Christmas
was the only time I even noticed that the whole world was
not Jewish. Suddenly, programs about Jesus appeared on
television and Santas showed up on street corners.
When I asked my parents why we couldn't celebrate
Christmas, they explained that we were Jews, and Jews
don't believe in Jesus.

Living in such a Jewish community, everything we did
seemed "normal"—not necessarily Jewish. Bagels and
lox and whitefish were a Sunday ritual in our house;
challah (still my favorite food), chicken soup and gefilte
fish were abundant on Friday evenings, and we were
never allowed to mix milk with meat. (I never understood
this to be a religious observance—my mother simply said
it would make my stomach sick.)

Every year we drove to Brooklyn to celebrate Passover
with my mother's family. My great aunt Lil had to
rearrange her entire dining and living rooms to seat more
than 20 of us. I remember vividly how difficult it was to

concentrate on the whole seder service while smelling the
tzimmes (a fruit and vegetable stew) from the kitchen.

Every year someone suggested that we skip parts of
the seder and move straight to dinner. Despite the
distraction of the tantalizing aromas, I always sided with
the family members fighting to go through the whole
service. I was also the only child willing to recite the
four questions, even after my younger sister Patti was old
enough to say them.

In that respect, I often found myself in the minority.
My father was raised Orthodox, but he and my mother
raised us in a Conservative Jewish home. Dad always
wanted to go back to the Orthodox synagogue for High
Holiday services, and when I was seven or eight years old
I started to go with him. Nobody else was interested, but
somehow, that *shul* felt more "holy" to me. Maybe it was
because people at the other synagogues often seemed to be
chatting and looking at what everyone else was wearing
and such. The Orthodox seemed to take their faith more
seriously; the men wore *tallit* (a ritual fringed garment),
knew all the prayers and recited them from beginning to
end. They seemed less interested in socializing and more
interested in God.

All this fascinated me because I truly wanted to
connect with God, whom I pictured as a gentle old man
living in the clouds. My mother had always told me that
heaven was up in the clouds. She also said that her
mother, who died before I was born, looked down from
heaven and watched over us. I'll never forget my first

airplane ride. I was about seven years old, and was
terribly disappointed when my grandmother's face did not
appear as we soared through the clouds!

I never doubted that God existed. I knew that he
talked to Abraham, Isaac and Jacob, and I was sad that
he did not talk to me—though I tried initiating
conversations. I loved God and wanted to please him. I
hoped to do so by lighting Shabbat candles, going to
Temple, learning prayers and "living right." But I knew
that I fell short of what he expected of me. I knew I
wasn't perfect, I didn't pray enough and of course we did
not follow all of the laws. I therefore did not blame him
for his silence. After all, halfway through the Orthodox
services I was bored and regretted having come with my
father. What must God think of that? I remember
leaving synagogue on Yom Kippur, wondering if God had
forgiven me.

My mother often joked that one day I would marry a
rabbi because, even as a child, I always said I was going
to read through the whole Bible. Despite many noble
attempts to do so, somehow I never made it past Leviticus.

I began Hebrew school in second grade. I had a major
crush on our cantor; he chanted the Hebrew so
beautifully, and he always had a cheerful grin and a hug
for me.

I also had a Hebrew teacher, Mr. Cohen, whom I did
not like very much. I remember telling my mother that
he wasn't a very kind man, and she suggested that I talk
to him after class and get to know him. So one day I did.

As we talked, he rolled up his sleeve and I saw numbers tattooed on his arm. He told me how his wife was killed in a concentration camp. Mr. Cohen was the first Holocaust survivor I ever met. I felt bad that I hadn't been kinder to him.

Around that time, our family saw a movie about the Holocaust together. In one scene, a crowd of naked people were gathered in a room. My father explained that they were being prepared for what they thought were showers, but that they were really going into gas chambers to die. "That's what the Gentiles will do to the Jews," he explained. From then on I knew that we Jews needed to stick together, and that we must never allow something like the Holocaust to happen again.

As sobering as this was, I was generally happy. I could hardly wait as my bat mitzvah approached. I recalled the gift my uncle Dave had given my older brother when he was a bar mitzvah. I absolutely adored Uncle Dave. He was the principal of a Hebrew school, and seemed to know everything. He could lead the prayers and, like me, he always wanted to do the whole seder. He gave my brother a huge Bible, with a gold cover. Right in the center of the cover was a beautiful picture of a Torah scroll.

I couldn't wait to have a Bible like Warren's. I had no idea that my parents, my grandfather and all the great aunts and uncles had ridiculed Uncle Dave's gift. They felt it was not appropriate for a modern 13-year-old. As a result, he gave me something else. I don't even remember

what it was, only that I was extremely disappointed.
(Years later, my brother gave me his Bible as a gift. It still
has a prominent place on my bookshelf today.)

That year, I was in synagogue every Shabbat—for the
bar and bat mitzvahs of all my friends. Most people I
knew endured the long services for the party that
followed, but I sought a connection to God during those
times. Even if I didn't know what all the Hebrew words
meant, I could follow the *siddur*, and I was proud of the
fact that I knew the liturgy.

I was awed to think that Jewish people around the
world were reciting the same words, at the same time, in
the same order as I was in Newton, Massachusetts (I was
not yet aware of time zones!). I loved feeling connected
to my people around the world. I knew that being Jewish
was special, that we were a chosen people.

Even so, after my bat mitzvah and graduation from
Hebrew school my involvement in synagogue deteriorated—
I only went on holidays and for special events, like
weddings. I was as Jewish as ever culturally, but I no
longer looked to Judaism for spiritual answers. It was the
late sixties, and drugs and Eastern religions suddenly
seemed very appealing.

When I was 16 I encountered the Jehovah's Witnesses
on a street corner, and agreed to allow them come to my
home. I still didn't know much about the Bible—except
for the stories I'd heard about King David and Elijah the
Prophet from Hebrew school. The Jehovah's Witnesses
talked about the Garden of Eden and sin. They raised a

question from one verse, then suggested turning to another verse to find the answer. I remember thinking the connection was questionable. I went to one of their meetings, and was very attracted to their joy. However, within three weeks of study, I concluded that what they were saying didn't make much sense.

The following summer I tried my hand at Scientology, partly because I had a crush on a guy who was into that. I attended meetings a few times a week for two months. I learned about "getting clear." This term refers to ridding oneself of all the negative garbage instilled in us over the years. I also learned to manipulate circumstances to get my own way, to convince people to do things against their will. I tried out this technique when I wanted a sales clerk to change her mind about selling me only one part of a two piece set. It worked! At that point, I realized I was dealing with a power that I was not equipped to handle. While Scientology seemed to offer solutions, they were not the spiritual solutions I was seeking. In fact, the solutions catered to the very selfishness I wanted to overcome.

During college I studied Eastern religions, both in class and on my own. Buddhism attracted me the most for several reasons. I liked the idea of breaking the cycle of bondage and achieving nirvana through my own efforts. The fact that Buddhism treats men and women as equals made it even more appealing.

I was no longer thinking about pleasing or displeasing God; I was just looking for something meaningful, and something that would help me deal with my fears.

For some reason, fear often seemed to dominate my life. As a child, and well into my teens, I was terrified of fire. As a young adult, I was afraid to leave my apartment. I imagined my car breaking down and leaving me stranded, or that someone would break into my apartment while I was gone and wait to harm me when I returned. Most of all, I was afraid that I wouldn't be able to support myself and live a functional life.

I doubt that anyone knew how fearful I was; I managed to hide my anxieties under a covering of success. I graduated from the University of Vermont with a B.A. in sociology, entered the professional world and established myself in the health care industry. Yet, secretly I feared that people would somehow discover that I wasn't as smart or as capable as the positions I held warranted.

In 1984 I was working on a Ph.D. in health care policy at Brandeis University. Fearing I wouldn't pass an economics class I was taking, I hired Chris—one of the brightest students in the class—to tutor me. We eventually formed a study group to prepare for our comprehensive exams.

One night, after our study time, Chris and I got into a discussion about abortion. As a Jewish woman from Massachusetts, I was pro-choice, of course. I was surprised to learn that Chris was what he called pro-life (a view I had only seen as anti-choice prior to our discussion). When I asked why on earth he took such a stance, he told me that he was a Christian.

I was 32 years old and had never met anyone who confessed to being a Christian. To think that such a

talented scholar would take the Bible so seriously
captured my attention. I had accepted the common belief
that the Bible is a mixture of Jewish history, myth and
good moral teaching, but not the word of God. It was
startling to think that someone as intelligent as Chris
would take the Bible literally.

What impressed me about Chris even more than his
intelligence was his peace. He was always calm. I never
saw him waver in his faith. He knew that God existed, he
knew that God was the God of the Bible, and he knew
why he believed what he believed. In fact, he knew more
about my Bible and more about Jewish history than I did.
He knew things that I felt I should have known as a Jew.
I was jealous of the peace he had, yet I knew that what he
believed couldn't be for me—because I was Jewish.

When Chris showed me the fifty-third chapter from
the prophet Isaiah, I could not believe that I was seeing
something from the Jewish Scriptures. As soon as I got
home I checked my own Bible. Sure enough, the passage
Chris had read was the same. I was amazed by how
clearly it seemed to describe the Christian view of Jesus.

Still, I looked for ways to challenge Chris and his
faith. Once I asked him, "Tell me, do you REALLY
believe that God created the world like the Bible says?"
Chris calmly replied, "Absolutely, don't you?" Then he
challenged me in turn: "And do you REALLY believe
that an amoeba jumped out of a puddle of water and
eventually became you? Tell me, which do you think
takes more faith?" That made me think.

And then one day, in the fall of 1988, a famous televangelist announced that if people didn't send him six million dollars for his ministry, God would "take him home" (in other words he would die if he didn't get the money). Soon after, Jim and Tammy Bakker were implicated in the PTL scandal. I figured this would give me the upper hand with Chris regarding faith issues. I marched into his office with a newspaper article about the Bakkers and said, "Okay, Chris, explain that." Still, he didn't waver. He simply said, "Karol, these are just people. People will always fall and make mistakes. Don't judge Jesus by what people do; judge Jesus by what Jesus did." That was the last time I challenged him.

In the meantime, I saw an ad in the *Boston Globe* from a group called Jews for Jesus. They offered a free book called *Testimonies*, which I ordered. I was shocked to read about Jews who actually believed in Jesus. Some time later, Jews for Jesus sent a letter asking if I wanted further information, and I ordered a booklet called *Questions and Answers*. I also indicated that I would be willing to talk with someone from Jews for Jesus.

Neither my discussions with Chris nor the books convinced me that Jesus was my Messiah. But in 1987 I faced a problem that I knew I could not handle without God. And when I called out to him for help, I was amazed that he answered.

Despite various fears, I had proved to be pretty self-disciplined and competent in most areas of my life. But there was one area which always seemed to get the best of

me. Food. It was clearly an addiction and an obsession.
I could diet with the best of them . . . for a while, but
inevitably I would gain all the weight back and then
some. I continued to ride this roller coaster for many
years. Occasionally, I was a borderline anorexic, but
usually I was overeating. I was out of control.

A friend suggested that I go with her to an Overeaters
Anonymous meeting. From my first meeting I knew I was
a compulsive overeater, and that I would never be able to
handle my problem by my own strength and willpower.
This program suggested certain steps toward a solution.
The first three involved:

1. Admitting that I was powerless over food and
    that my life had become unmanageable.
2. Realizing that a power greater than myself
    could restore me, and
3. Turning my will and my life over to the care of
    God as I understood him.

I had already taken the first step. As for the second
step, I already knew that God existed, but I wasn't sure
that he would help me.

Nevertheless, the next day I asked God for his help.
The people at the program said that I'd need to abstain
from sugar and flour to break the eating cycle. So that is
what I asked God to help me do: abstain from eating sugar
or flour for one day, just one day. At the end of the day,
God had answered my prayer—talk about a miracle!

Day after day God continued to answer my prayer and
help me do what I could not do for myself. I soon
realized that God could and would restore me completely,
if I would turn my will and life over to him. I began to
pray every morning, "God, show me your will for me and I
promise I'll do it—no questions asked." It was during
one such prayer that I felt a tug on my heart: "What are
you going to do about Jesus?"

I wondered if the tug was from God. I felt certain that
the Jewish God would not want me to believe in Jesus,
but I decided to ask him about it. For three weeks
straight, every morning I asked God to show me if Jesus
was really the Messiah. I also prayed that if Jesus was
not the Messiah, that God would protect me from
believing in him and thus committing idolatry.

The truth is, I was afraid to believe in Jesus because I
knew that if I did, my friends and family would consider me
an outsider and a traitor. I was also concerned about other
ramifications. I remember asking Chris, "If I believe in
Jesus, do I have to change my political views?" He
responded, "The only thing you have to believe is that Jesus
died for your sin and rose from the dead. The rest you don't
have to worry about now." When I weighed my fears
against the possibility of having a personal relationship with
the God of the universe, what choice did I have?

I'd been praying about this for three weeks when I
had lunch with Chris. At one point during our meal he
looked at me and said, "I think you are ready to accept
Jesus." In that moment I knew that I already had. A

week later, a man named Steve from Jews for Jesus
called in response to the card I'd sent a few months
earlier. Coincidence?

"I can't believe you're calling now," I said to him.
"I just came to believe in Jesus, and I don't know what
do next." Steve and I began to study the Bible together
weekly, and he was able to help me navigate some of
the questions and concerns I had as a Jewish believer
in Jesus.

Once I even handed out literature about Jesus in
downtown Boston. Having done so, I could not imagine
that I would ever go back out there, to stand on street
corners in the freezing cold and have people look at me
like I was crazy (or through me like I didn't exist). No
way. One evening Steve approached me and said, "I
think you might like to become a missionary with Jews for
Jesus." I remember my unspoken retort, "And I think
you must be crazy." Still, I agreed to pray about it, and
ask God what he wanted from me. After all, that was my
original prayer, that I would do what God wanted, no
questions asked.

While I was grateful for the role Steve had played in
my life, I had no desire to go and do likewise. I thought
that it would make much more sense for me to reach out
to addicts, or something of that nature, since God had
helped me with my food addiction.

Then I went to church one Sunday, and the pastor's
message, from Isaiah 54, was about missions. I knew that
God was telling me to bring the good news I'd received to

my own people. In fact, it was such a strong sense that it was almost as if the finger of God was poking me in the chest, as he clearly said, "YOU!" I half expected the whole church to turn around and stare as God was speaking to me. Somewhat embarrassed, I finally said to God, "Okay, okay, I hear you!"

I joined the staff of Jews for Jesus in 1990. That July, I went to New York City with 25 or so Jewish believers from around the country. As is tradition with Jews for Jesus, we had come to spend a month handing out literature on street corners and talking to people about Jesus.

I was terrified to approach complete strangers, especially in Times Square at night! I expressed my anxiety to a more experienced member of my team, and he left me on a corner with three police officers, hoping their presence would make me feel safer. It didn't.

I could have asked God for courage to tell people about my faith that night, but I must confess that instead I prayed, "God you are the creator of the universe and you can make me invisible." All I wanted was for the next two hours to pass quickly, without having to interact with anyone. But that is not what happened.

A tall, lanky street preacher came and stood a few feet from me. He opened his Bible and began to preach his heart out. And, as I heard the Scriptures preached, I felt a new joy and boldness. A young woman saw my Jews for Jesus T-shirt and stopped to talk. I asked if I could tell her about Jesus. By the end of our conversation she was ready to ask God to give her a new life based on forgiveness through Jesus! It was the first time I had ever seen someone come to faith before my very eyes. When she went away that night, I owned that corner, and actively and eagerly looked for anyone else that I could talk to about Jesus. It wasn't long before I realized that all of the police officers were gone, and so was my street preacher . . . and so was my fear. And that fear has never, ever returned!

Shalom at Last
An Israeli's Journey to Jesus

by Shlomy Abramov

It is not every day that a *sabra* (an Israeli-born Jew) sees that the Messiah of Israel is none other than Y'shua, Jesus Christ. Here is my story.

I am of the Kurdish Jews,* the ones Saddam Hussein tried to wipe out with mustard gas in the late 1980s.

Just as the Eastern European Jews (Ashkenazi) were persecuted by Hitler and his kind, the Sephardic Jews have faced blind hatred in the Arabic countries in which we have

lived. The persecution was extremely dangerous for my
grandfather in the mountains of Kurdistan. He feared for his
family's life, and longed for Israel as all Jews do. He brought
the family to Israel in 1933. My father was four months old.

My mother is a fourth generation Israeli with Kurdish and
Turkish roots. She grew up in Rishon le Zion, Israel. Rishon
le Zion, which means "the first to Zion," describes my mother's
family, who came to Israel before the rebirth of the state. My
mother remembers when life was different in the Promised
Land—innocent. These days she tries to make me promise I
will not travel, being fearful I will run into terrorism.

My parents met through my mother's brother. He and
my dad were friends. Every day after school my dad would
pass through their garden on the way home. Mom was 15
and Dad was 20 when they fell in love. The family asked
him to marry Hanna, the elder sister, but his heart was for
my mother—not unlike Jacob and Rachel. (The culture
says to marry the older one first always. When they wanted
to marry, Mom lied about her age because she was too
young legally!) When my mother's family saw that my
father would not change his mind about which daughter to
court, they agreed to the marriage. My parents married in
1955 and are still married to this day.

I was born in Israel in 1959. I have two sisters, Roslyn
and Tamara, and one brother, Ilon. I have numerous
uncles and aunts, so many in fact that my wife jokes that
we are the 13th tribe of Israel.

My boyhood was not unusual. Israel is no different

than many other places where boys engage in small rivalries and neighborhood fights. But in Israel we learned a more serious enmity for those who seemed determined to hate and destroy us. We grew up wanting to fight our enemies, the Arabs—well, I did especially.

I was a good student all through school and particularly excelled in Torah (Bible) and in singing—probably because I enjoyed them so much. We sang lots of folk songs, mainly about *Eretz Yisrael* (the Land of Israel). We all learned to appreciate and love our land very deeply. I felt a great oneness with the land and the people when we sang. I loved being able to express my own feelings for Israel through music.

We also learned about the Bible from an early age. Perhaps God chose Abraham knowing that he would teach his children, and their children's children and so on. Perhaps that is why we learn about the Bible at a young age, even today. I don't think anyone will throw the Bible out of Israel's school system the way they have elsewhere.

Along with the Bible lessons, we learned about the holidays. The holiday I recall most vividly is not commanded in the Bible, but is based on the book of Esther. That is Purim, when we commemorate how the Jews were saved from wicked Haman. It is a joyous celebration of survival, during which children dress up in costumes. It is also a holiday for pranks and humor, almost like April Fool's Day. One year at my school they had all the little boys dress up in ballerina costumes and asked us to twirl for the whole school and parents' assembly. They especially wanted boys with chubby, hairy legs—that was me!

A man at 13?

I began attending synagogue at age five; every weekend I went faithfully with my father. As I got older, the weekly synagogue services were supplemented with lessons to prepare me for my bar mitzvah.

The bar mitzvah is a Jewish rite of passage into manhood at age 13. The bar mitzvah boy leads the worship service, saying the Hebrew prayers, reading a portion of Scripture from the Hebrew scroll, and addressing the audience with a brief homily.

For my big day, I recited the first chapter of Jeremiah. I had studied hard, learning to read the Hebrew words and also how to sing them exactly as the rabbi taught me. When the day came, I was able to show how well I had learned and my whole family was very proud. As was our custom, everyone threw candy to symbolize God's sweetness and the goodness of his Torah. After the service, all the children ran to gather the small pieces of candy.

So I became a man at 13—at least in the traditional sense—and my father was ecstatic. I can still remember his face. He had big plans for me to be religious, like my uncle, who is a big shot in the local *Beit Knesset* (synagogue). Sephardic Israelis rarely go against their parents' wishes. We are expected to do what the tribe leader, that is the father, wants. And I did attend synagogue quite regularly for a while.

I wanted to please my father; nevertheless, things began to change after the bar mitzvah. Friends challenged me, asking if I had seen God. Next they wanted to know how I could believe if I hadn't seen him. I became stubborn and I began to doubt God; I wanted to "see" God because of what my friends said to me. So I asked God to show himself to me. As I lay upon my bed one night I said, "Father in heaven, if you really exist then come down and show yourself to me; then I will believe you." I actually expected God to show himself, to come face-to-face with me. To my surprise no one came. I waited still, but no one came.

In my stubborn ignorance I concluded that because God did not "show up" at my demand, he must not exist. Within two months of my bar mitzvah I stopped going to synagogue altogether.

A real man now, army days

Service in the army is mandatory for all Israelis, women and men. I faithfully enlisted for my duty at age 18. I was hoping to be a great fighter. I wanted to avenge Israel—as do many 18-year-olds—to "pay back" our enemies for each life that had been taken. To my disappointment I was instead assigned to manage a warehouse on the base! The only fighting for me was fighting my own frustration as I folded clothes and kept lists of everything going out of the warehouse, from gardening tools to tanks.

It was not such a bad assignment, really. I supervised

many people and delegated authority. People came to me
for everything from uniforms and shoelaces to tools and
weapons. Everyone, it seemed, wanted to be my friend
because I could get them what they wanted. They gave
me the best of the food in the mess hall and it made me
feel important. When my mandatory service ended, I
continued for another year, in officer's training. I then
applied for the police academy. I was accepted and
became an officer in Rishon le Zion, my hometown.

I really enjoyed being part of the police force,
especially in the beginning. I patrolled neighborhoods
and did crime investigation. I broke down doors of
suspicious people. I also did some undercover work. I
felt respected. I loved the work so much that I
volunteered many overtime hours for free!

However, there were aspects of the job I found
discouraging. Some of my co-workers seemed tougher
than what I thought was necessary, and there were those
who were out for themselves rather than the people they
were serving. I think this is a problem faced by police
forces the world over. It is tempting to allow oneself to be
corrupted by the power.

Looking back, I realize that I had a strong desire for
righteousness without even knowing it. Deep down I was
hungry for good things, honest people. My soul was dry and
I thirsted for spiritual truth. I resigned from the force and
went into high-level private security work.

I became sought out as a good bodyguard; some in
Israel have said I was the best. My first jobs were in

nightclubs featuring celebrity entertainers. Always there would be some drunk trying to get close enough to touch the famous singer. I made sure they kept their distance. I enjoyed feeling respected and needed, and it made me feel important to guard some of Israel's most famous people. I earned the nickname "Rambo" while playing an extra in Sylvester Stallone's *Rambo 3* that was filming in the Holy Land. It was a good nickname for a bodyguard.

Whenever an Arab/Israeli fight broke out at a concert or in a bar, I was called onto the scene. I also had the privilege of protecting the late Prime Minister Isaac Shamir as well as Ariel Sharon. And I was the manager of security for the sports stadium in Jerusalem, Teddy Stadium. Everybody in Israel is a sports fan, so I made lots of friends. Occasionally, people who remember me from those days will still say, "Hi, Rambo," when they see me on the street.

These jobs were lucrative and gratifying to my ego . . . so why did I feel empty and frustrated? I could not find answers to life. I began searching for spiritual answers. One person told me to try tarot cards, another pointed me to astrology, and another still told me to have the grounds in my coffee cup read. I would see a sign on the street promising some spiritual awareness and I would go inside. Sometimes people told me things about myself or my life that were true, but there was nothing compelling about their words. I needed real truth and conviction, and I wasn't finding it.

The things I expected to make me happy were

somehow meaningless. I spent my 20s chasing after
things that could not satisfy me. I wished that God had
shown up as I, in my arrogance, had demanded at my bar
mitzvah. I went here and there, always hoping for some
touch, some interaction with God. I tried to forget by
drinking, but that only made things worse. After a while,
I could not even feel the effects of the alcohol. I had
drinking competitions with a friend, and more than once
we drank so much that I had to drive him to the hospital.
I was slipping very fast into darkness. The celebrity
nightclub scene only added to that darkness. In fact, they
fit together like a glove—a boxer's glove that was
readying for the knockout punch. I knew that I was
headed for a fall and there was no one to catch me.

God still didn't come. Was I still waiting?

When I reached my 30s my search brought me full
circle and I decided to go back to my roots. I began
attending the synagogue once more. One rainy day I
walked to the synagogue with my umbrella, which was
doubling as a cane following a surgery I'd had. As soon
as I entered, one member, a friend of my father's, began
yelling. In angry tones he told me that I was violating
the Sabbath and offending God by carrying the
umbrella. His words really stung, because I was trying
to find my way back to God. I had not intended to
offend him; moreover, I could not understand why God
would be offended for me to carry something as small as

an umbrella in order to keep myself dry as I entered to worship him. Was God really like that? I thought he was supposed to be a God of love. Was I a fool to seek out such a God?

A turn for the better

One day my good friend Danny asked me to go to Tiberius, on the Sea of Galilee, for the weekend. I was to bring my girlfriend and he would bring his wife. It was Rosh Hashanah, the Jewish New Year. But my girlfriend and I had a misunderstanding, and the next thing I knew she was breaking up with me. I was miserable and in no mood for a holiday, but I thought, "I am tough, I am Rambo, and I made a commitment to my friend." I told Danny that he could count on me to go to Galilee despite the circumstances.

We checked into our accommodations: a small mobile home on the *Kinneret* (Sea of Galilee). Then we went to the local kibbutz to buy food. It was a large kibbutz and we could not find the market. Finally, we asked someone with a kind face which way to go. She politely pointed us to the market. Later we saw her again, an attractive young woman with whom I wanted to strike up a conversation. We started talking and somehow the subject of God came up. Then she started telling me about Y'shua, whom she had the nerve to say was the Messiah of Israel. Further, she told me I needed to be pointed in his direction! I told her that I was a Jew, and an Israeli at that, and that Jesus is not in my vocabulary. Furthermore, I told her that if she were a man I

would break her in half. But Miriam was not the least bit
intimidated. She just kept talking about him.

Guess who's coming to dinner?

I was accustomed to having my way. Normally, if I asked
people to stop what they were doing, they did. I expected
the same of Miriam, and was pleasantly surprised. I
admired her nerve and we became friends. She was so
nice and polite, this girl, but she had a certain wisdom
and strength. She was very different from the other girls I
knew, which gave my parents cause to like her very
much. They invited her to Sabbath dinner every Friday
night, and funny things began to happen. Miriam would
talk about Y'shua, and would get my parents talking
about Y'shua, and their friends, too.

When my parents first realized I intended to marry
this woman, they were upset because of her faith in Jesus.
But when they saw how determined I was, and as they
came to love her for the very qualities I saw in her, they
softened. My mother assured me that this girl would
"come around," meaning she would turn her back on
Jesus so that we could get married. My father promised
he would give me his blessing when the time came, which
was very important to me.

And so Miriam continued to come and discuss Jesus
with whoever else was invited to our Shabbat dinners.
One of my father's friends even went so far as to say that
Jesus was King of the Jews. After all, he pointed out, they
crowned him as such on the cross, so why not just be

Jewish and leave out the part about him being Messiah?
At that moment something moved in my parents' hearts:
he was King of the Jews, hmmmm, they pondered—
interesting how he was crowned with that title at his death.
They had not heard that before.

God goes after me

I began to thirst for God all over again. In fact, I realized that
the thirst had never died; I had just pushed it aside. But with
Miriam the topic was always God, and she would not let me
push it aside. In fact, she gave me a New Testament to read.
At first I refused, but she knew I loved history and she
challenged me to read it as a historic book that has
influenced millions of people. She also challenged me to
read the Old Testament prophecies and compare them with
the New Testament. I agreed, confident that I could never be
deceived as long as I had my own Bible. Like many Jewish
people I had been taught that Christians twisted the Old
Testament to speak of Jesus. So I got out my own Bible and I
read and read. And I began to search with all my heart.

Miriam left Israel for six months. When she returned,
she would not see me, and I did not know why. Perhaps
she began to realize that my family and I were all hoping
for her to give up on Y'shua so I could marry her, and she
did not want to encourage such a false hope. At any rate, I
finally invited her to a family wedding. This she accepted.
Oh yes, and there was one other place she agreed to see
me . . . the Messianic assembly (of believers in Y'shua) at
Mount Carmel!

So because I wanted to see her, I came to the congregation. The warmth I felt there was amazing. Everyone was so friendly. Then they started to sing. I had always loved singing, but this music seemed somehow special. It drew me in as they sang about Jesus—but they called him Y'shua, which is how you pronounce it in Hebrew. By then I had begun to realize that the New Testament is, so, well . . . Jewish. I still didn't quite understand how that could be.

What I did understand was that I wanted very much to be with this girl, and also that I wanted to pay these nice people back for their kindness by doing something that would make them happy. At the end of the service they asked anyone who never knew Jesus' love and forgiveness for sins to come forward. I quickly seized this opportunity. Like Rambo, I pushed the chairs to each side and made my own path up the middle! I of course did not know any church etiquette. I repeated the prayer as the pastor invited us to do, to receive Jesus in my heart—not because I was fully convinced, but because I saw it as a kindness that I could do for these people whose love and good will I so appreciated.

World War III: internal struggle

I got home that night and found myself with a new internal struggle on my hands. My own thoughts seemed to storm against me. You are a Jew, what have you done? Your family will kill you. As a Kurdish Sephardic Jew I could not imagine doing something that would be so mortifying to my family. I didn't know what to do.

I continued to attend the congregation. I felt embraced with arms of love whenever I came. I never had felt like this before. These people showed genuine concern and they drew closer to me than most people in my circles. Their love for me combined with my love for Torah to keep me coming back.

And I found myself doing something I had not done for a long time. I went back to reading my Bible. I read for hours, for days. I came across the part I had learned for my bar mitzvah. God knew me before I was even in my mother's womb. He knows me still. Suddenly, as I read, a bizarre thing happened. As I held the Bible, it was as if a person appeared, walking out of the pages, coming closer and closer to me. It occurred to me that Y'shua himself was alive and stepping out of the pages of the Bible.

I was stunned. I felt as though a ten-ton brick had struck me. I realized that I'd had a very personal encounter with the Son of the living God. That whole week I was dumbstruck.

The following week I returned to Miriam's congregation, and this time when the pastor asked if anyone wanted to know Jesus in his heart, I answered the call—not because I wanted to make the people of the congregation happy, but because I knew who Y'shua was: my messiah, a Jew who was more than a man, God in the flesh. He died because of my sin, but he rose from the dead. I understood that he came to be my atonement, if I would recognize my sin and my need for

him. I had no thoughts of Miriam or the other friends
I'd made as I went forward to receive him.

A few weeks later I realized something as I recalled my
bar mitzvah and how I had demanded that God show himself
to me. Twenty years later he did exactly that. Twenty years
is nothing to the eternal God. He was so gracious to help me
understand his truth at a time when I was ready. Hope
welled up inside of me. What a feeling, to know that God is
alive, and he is real. He heard me 20 years earlier and he
was with me all the time. The 20 years I had waited for him
were as less than a second from his perspective! I know that
he will be with me forever.

A postscript or two

Miriam, the woman who first shared Y'shua with me,
became my wife. We went on to graduate from Israel
College of the Bible, where we each obtained a four-year
degree in Bible. I became the first sabra to obtain a
Bachelor of Theology degree in the history of the College.

My wife (who is also an Israeli citizen) and I now work
with Jews for Jesus to share the hope of our Messiah
throughout Israel. And I have a little story to tell about that.

Shortly before I received Y'shua as my Messiah, I told
my good friend Ronnie about a strange dream I had. I
dreamed I was standing in a little building with a Moorish
style window. I looked down and saw a beautiful picture
at my feet, with some writing that I couldn't quite read.

The time came for me to be baptized. (Contrary to what
many people think, baptism is not a renouncing of one's

Jewish heritage, but an affirmation of one's identity with the Jewish Messiah.) I went to the Jordan River with my congregation and was baptized there with another believer named Avi. My friend Ronnie, who knew of my dream, was present. He told me he had a surprise for me.

After the baptism we all walked up to the small chapel at the YMCA and sat in the pews. The pastor asked me to tell how I came to believe in Jesus. I walked to the front of the chapel. As I searched for words to share with the group, I looked at the floor for a moment. And that's when I saw it. It was the same picture I had seen in my dream, and then as I looked up I noticed the Moorish arch, the window that I had also seen months earlier in the dream. I was stunned beyond words.

Some time after, my wife insisted we go back and see what was written. (She was not present at my baptism.) You see, the writing was in English and, well . . . I speak Hebrew.

So we went to the Galilee where I was baptized, back to the little chapel. There we saw the words on the floor where I had stood. They told about a man who had given his whole life for the service of the Lord. It was at that moment I realized that God was calling me to serve him just as he had called the man described in the writing. Why else had God given me this dream? It made up for 20 years of waiting.

Speaking of the baptism, it was a show of God's power in more than one way. You see, I was baptized with a Palestinian (Tassir is his name). It is unusual to see close friendships between Jews and Arabs in Israel these days.

In my family, for instance, my mother and father each lost
a brother in the fight for Israel's independence. We all
have friends, or friends of friends, who have died in
terrorist attacks. But I found that when people come to
Y'shua, they change. I changed. God softened my heart
so that I love my Arab brothers and sisters who know
Y'shua, and I can have the compassion to pray for those
who don't.

One last thing I want you to know. My mother came to
faith in Y'shua in 2004! For ten years she had heard of
Messiah from me. She got to the point where she began
asking for prayer for her own health, as well as my dad's, in
Jesus' name. She watched God answer various prayers for
family members over the years. In particular, when my
niece was having severe emotional problems, Miriam and I
asked our supporters to pray for her. They did and she was
restored! That touched my mother's heart for the Lord.

All this brought her to a point where she was willing
to come along when we invited her to a special prayer
meeting. This in itself was an answer to prayer because
when she told my father she was planning to go, he said,
"How can you leave me on the Sabbath?!" You see, in 50
years she had never left the house on the Sabbath.

This is a deep tradition here, not at all uncommon
among my people. But Mom told Dad that I had tickets to
this special meeting. She had lots of pain in her leg and
had gone to rabbis for help with no success. They told her
wear a ribbon on her wrist, they suggested she cook certain
concoctions, lay things under her pillow at night and

various other superstitions. Clearly, nothing worked. She was ready to ask Y'shua for help. She not only attended the function with us, but also went forward at the altar call to repent of sin and receive Jesus. Hallelujah!

If you are a believer in Y'shua, I hope you have been encouraged to see how God brought this sabra to know him. If you have not believed in Y'shua but are considering him, I hope that you will ask God to show you the truth.

Endnote

* The Kurds were among those helping American forces in Iraq to find Hussein. They also assisted in sealing the border in Northern Iraq, helping to topple his regime.

Loss to Life

A Jewish Woman's Journey to Messiah

by Susan Perlman

We piled onto a special bus destined for a big march in Washington D.C., a group of friends and strangers united by one purpose. We were protesters, heading for the Pentagon, our nation's military headquarters. While this was serious business, the mood on board was light and festive. People chatted and joked. Now and then someone would burst into song and others would join in.

When we reached the halfway point between New York City and Washington, D.C., the bus pulled into a

highway rest stop/restaurant. Everyone made a beeline
for the restrooms and, as is often the case, the line for the
women's room was much longer than the line for the
men's. Suddenly, I had a brainstorm: "Why not liberate
the men's room?" I expressed my idea to the women
waiting next to me. Their enthusiasm helped me muster
the courage to lead an onslaught on the men's room. We
"stormed" the door and successfully "liberated" the men's
room, making it coed—much to the astonishment of the
restaurant's proprietors, not to mention the bewildered
men who were inside!

That small act of courage and creativity bolstered my
confidence as I stepped back on the bus. People
continued to chat, sing and laugh right up to the time the
familiar monuments of our nation's capital came into
view. Then the tension, the uneasiness began to set in.
There was always the possibility of violence during
such demonstrations and I, for one, did not want to be
maced or get my head bashed in.

Ironically, like the police we expected to face, we had
our own uniform of sorts: faded denim jeans, T-shirts and
sandals—though the more experienced protesters wore
closed-toed shoes. I began to cringe as I saw some
people donning homemade riot regalia that seemed
almost to invite attack: motorcycle helmets, construction
hard hats. Their assorted gear seemed out of place in a
march for peace! Did they know something that I didn't?

Our little contingent converged with thousands of

others in an open area where a platform had been
erected. A long program of speakers and folk singers
took their turns at the microphone, but what I remember
most is the march that followed. We began with the
chant, "All we are saying, is give peace a chance," which
we repeated over and over. Then the slogans became
more strident, more clipped, "Ho, Ho, Ho Chi Minh,
N.L.F. is gonna win!" I remember crossing over the area
marked "No trespassing." In the distance, we could see
the Pentagon, the symbol of our nation's military might.
We could hear the tactical police with their bullhorns,
warning marchers that they would be arrested if they
continued in that direction.

At that moment, part of me wished that I was not on
the line of march. But I had no chance of retreat as the
crowd pushed forward. I felt the burning sensation of tear
gas in my eyes. I saw the police attacking marchers and I
saw some marchers attacking the police. It was ugly.
Then everyone started running. There was no longer a
line of march, just hundreds, no, thousands of people
scattering in all directions. Shouts of, "Off the pigs! Off
the pigs!" were met with clubs and counter slogans like
"Draft-dodging commies!" I was not a shouter, but I was
sure a runner, only I wasn't exactly sure what direction I
was going with all the shoving and hitting and pummeling.

I finally found a bench. I sat down, dazed.

It wasn't until later that I had time to reflect on the
day's events. We'd gone to Washington for a noble and

just cause. We saw ourselves as the voice of sanity in an insane world. We were protesting what we believed to be an unjust war in Vietnam. I knew that it was beyond my ability to truly comprehend the human carnage going on over there, even though I watched the news clips on TV and listened to the death toll broadcast every night. I remember thinking how sick the world must be if words like "a just and honorable peace" were considered more important than life itself. Was it "honorable" for people to be napalmed to death? I felt I had to raise my voice to protest this evil. So there I was, part of a peace demonstration that had turned into a hostile, bloody mess.

I survived the march on the Pentagon, but I was never the same. I rode back on the bus later that same day. It wasn't as full. Some had stayed on, perhaps not by choice, I thought. There was light chatter in the bus, even some laughter. I found myself resenting the mood as I remained silent. I felt so helpless, unable (at least for the moment) to do anything that would really make a difference.

All too often "might" triumphed over "right," and a few people in high places made decisions that affected the rest of us—decisions in which we had no voice or choice. This was particularly frustrating to me as a person who values choice. This is a fact, family and friends tell me, that I made apparent at a very early age.

A case in point happened in kindergarten. As a toddler, I spent a lot of time with an elderly-uncle from Eastern Europe. He was a favorite uncle of mine and quite naturally, I picked up his accent so that when I started school, I would say words like "vat" instead of "what" and "vye" instead of "why." The teacher was somewhat puzzled at my accent, given that I was born in Brooklyn, New York. And once I realized how different I sounded from the other kids, I worked hard to rid myself of that European accent. By first grade, I had replaced it with my accent of choice—Brooklynese.

In fact, if I could have chosen where to be born, I would have! Though I was in no position to make that choice, I feel that my parents made the right choice for me—Beth El Hospital in Brooklyn. The hospital was later renamed "Brookdale"—probably for someone who donated a large sum of money—but I still like to think of it as Beth El, which means "House of God."

I didn't choose the neighborhood in Brooklyn where I grew up, but I assumed that everyone else who lived there was Jewish like me. After all, our schools were closed on the Jewish holidays. All our teachers had names like Mrs. Katz and Mrs. Epstein. Our merchants were also Jewish, like Mr. Sol Warren, the pharmacist and Mr. Pincus, the grocer. We didn't know from O'Rourkes or Smiths in our neighborhood. We never saw Christmas decorations or Easter bunnies or other "Christian" symbols unless we wandered out of the neighborhood to places like Manhattan, where the big Christmas tree was erected at Rockefeller Center each December.

I was aware that non-Jews existed. I even had a Gentile friend who didn't live in the neighborhood, but who attended my school. Her name was Priscilla Sanchez.

One day, she approached me at the school playground with the accusation, "I learned this week that you killed Jesus!" She was very upset and so was I. I protested, but after all, her instruction came from an adult, a religious teacher, and I was just a kid. People our age naturally trusted adults to be smarter and wiser—especially those in authority, like rabbis and priests and ministers. I could do nothing to convince Priscilla of my innocence.

From then on, we'd acknowledge each other with a glance now and then, but we never played together again. That made me sad, but I also remember thinking what a crazy religion Christians must have if they taught lies about little Jewish girls killing "their god."

I knew that being Jewish was a good thing. I was particularly proud of my heritage when, at age eight, I was chosen to play the part of Queen Esther in the local Purim pageant put on by the Young Women's Hebrew Association. As I recited my lines from the stage of the YM-YWHA, I was Queen Esther, the fairest maiden in all of Shushan. My flowing white robe with specks of glued-on glitter and my crown, though only made of cardboard and dime store gems, truly made me feel like this historic heroine of my people. My family and friends smiled proudly from the very front row. The play became a wonderful, magical experience and a trace of that glow still warms me whenever I recall it.

Yet my connection as a Jew with the God of the Jews was somewhat fuzzy. I didn't think much about God, other than the fact that he existed. Then when I was twelve, my father died of a heart attack. It was very sudden and unexpected and our family was in shock. Most children don't have to come to grips with the weighty issues of life and death, but I did—and so did my two younger sisters. I thought very intensely about the fact that life was so transitory. I wondered about what happens to us when we die.

The funeral was a bit of a blur to me. But afterwards, as is customary in the Orthodox Jewish tradition of mourning, our family spent a week sitting *shiva* (*shiva* means seven). We were not allowed to leave the apartment at any time during that week. There were many other restrictions such as not looking at one's own image (mirrors are therefore covered in the home) and refraining from all work or business. Mourners are not supposed to bathe, wash their clothes, cut their hair or even study the Bible—if they were so inclined.

I remember during that week of mourning, we sat on wooden crates in the living room. Many relatives and friends came to visit us, bringing food and recalling their fondest memories of my dad. I hardly knew the rabbi who made the obligatory visit to my house. At the funeral he'd spoken of my father's virtues, but his words were empty to me—mostly gathered from the questions he asked our family just prior to the service.

I didn't blame the rabbi for not knowing my father. My dad only went to *shul* (synagogue) for the High Holiday services and for special events. He sat way in the back so the rabbi never had the occasion to know

him. But I did have a pressing question to ask the rabbi.
So when he came to visit as we sat shiva, I boldly asked,
"Rabbi, is my daddy in heaven?" He paused, not
expecting the question, but his smile seemed reassuring.
"Susan, your father's memory will live on in the life you
lead. You can be his legacy." It was a nice thought, but
it didn't satisfy me. "Rabbi," I went on, ". . . you didn't
answer my question. Is my daddy in heaven now?" He
was a little more serious at this point and looked straight
into my eyes and said, "I wish I could give you a definite
answer, Susan, but I can't. We don't know for sure what is
beyond the grave. We can only hope. And remember,
your father was a good man."

The rabbi's second attempt at an answer troubled me
even more. I couldn't articulate why it concerned me
then. In retrospect, I think I was dismayed by his
uncertainty about something as fundamental to religion—
his area of expertise, after all—as an afterlife. "How
come we 'can't know for sure'?" I thought.

One thing I did know at the time was that I was
bewildered. How could a great, all-powerful God allow
this to happen? Didn't he know that my father was a good
man? He was only 38 years old—couldn't God see that
my mother, my two sisters and I needed my dad? I was
angry with God, yet paradoxically, I questioned whether
or not he was even real. Maybe he only existed in my
imagination and in the traditions of our religion. I had to
admit that even the rabbi seemed a little uncertain about
anything supernatural.

Regardless of whether or not God existed, my positive feelings about my Jewishness remained strong. I reasoned that if I was going to believe in God at all or be a religious person, I would certainly not be anything other than Jewish. In comparison to my concept of Christianity, I felt ours was the more practical, responsible religion. I viewed Christianity according to what I had seen in movies: a killer walks into a confession booth to spill his guts to the priest, he lists all his crimes, then simply tells how he wants to make a new start. The priest says, "My son, you are forgiven," makes him say a few prayers, and that's that. How convenient! Way too easy. Nope, it just didn't seem right to me.

On the other hand, I felt Judaism taught people to take responsibility for their own actions. It seemed lame to cry to God when I did something wrong. Likewise, I reasoned it was false humility to give God credit when I did something right. I felt satisfied that I had come to a balanced understanding of such things. I really worked hard at doing things "right," at least, according to my own perception of "rightness."

I was an above-average student and rapidly advanced through junior and senior high. During that time I was in a sorority, on the cheering squad, assistant coach for the boy's swim team, wrote for the yearbook and was captain of the student patrol. I graduated from high school in a January term and had a one-week break before entering college less than a month after my sixteenth birthday.

I had enrolled in Hunter College in Manhattan for a

four-year nursing program. Unlike the liberal arts
students, I was able to live in a dormitory. My mother was
concerned about my leaving home at such a young age, for
even though Manhattan was not that far from Brooklyn, it
was really a whole new world, and I would be out on my
own. To me it was a great opportunity, a real adventure.

I turned out to be one of two Jews in the entire nursing
program; everyone else seemed to be Irish Catholic. It
was a strange sensation to be in the minority. Yet Gail,
the other Jewish student, was right next door to me in the
dorm, and we took comfort in having each other nearby.
We talked often, but it wasn't the same as being in
Brooklyn. Life in the nursing dorm was a far cry from the
Brooklyn neighborhood where I grew up. And that was
particularly evident at Christmastime. The lobby of the
building where we lived was almost all glass windows,
and the students traditionally decorated them with
holiday scenes using a white frost-like spray paint.
While almost everyone was busy designing their holly
wreaths, jingle bells and jolly old Santas, I was given a
window all my own and felt a responsibility to Jewish
people everywhere as I defiantly drew a Hanukkah
menorah. Just to be sure people understood that this was
a Jewish window pane, I included a rather large Star of
David as well. My "Jewish corner" was there lest anyone
think that there were only Irish Catholics in our dorm.

I didn't last too long in the nursing program, but it
didn't have anything to do with my being Jewish. I quickly
discovered that I had more aptitude and interest in my

liberal arts classes than in the courses nursing required, as demonstrated by my poor science grades. Not only that, but I was quite squeamish around blood and I could not seem to be objective in my response to people's pain. I was strongly affected by suffering, as nurses should be, but I could not distance myself as nurses must. I remember coming back to my room from a day in the hospital feeling deeply depressed. "Why so much pain and suffering?" I agonized. Then I would cry myself to sleep. This happened frequently. Sadly, when I left the nursing program, I also had to leave the dorm. I had enjoyed the taste of independence and could not see myself moving back to my mother's apartment in Brooklyn.

It didn't take long to find roommates, and together we rented an apartment above "Poor Philip's Head Shop" on St. Mark's Place in Greenwich Village. The location was exotic in some ways, but after a few weeks I started taking on the same exotic appearance as my surroundings. My friends and family thought I looked weird and, to be honest, I did. I moved out of Greenwich Village and into an upper west side apartment with three other girls. We actually lived on the thirteenth floor of a very nice high-rise—but as is the custom in many such buildings, they had labeled it the fourteenth floor. It was an unusually large four-bedroom apartment that even included a "maid's room." The former tenants sold us their huge, carved oak dining room table and chairs as well as some other impressive pieces. The apartment had a real fireplace and was so spacious that it was perfect for lots of entertaining. And that we did. We were living well.

I continued with my studies, shifting my major to Communications. My roommates were all older than I, and fully employed. I did some waitressing to help pay the bills, but was still undecided about what I would do for a career. I saw myself as a cause-motivated, action-oriented independent woman. I continued to participate in marches like the one in Washington, D.C., and I never gave up my efforts to "make a difference." I was an active member of our neighborhood block association and worked toward building a sense of community. I helped raise funds for a dog run along Riverside Park (though I never owned a dog), and took part in a neighborhood recycling center for glass and aluminum. I even helped with hiring a security guard to discourage junkies and dope dealers from hanging out on our street.

I also became active in guerrilla theater (street drama) as a creative means of making social statements. One role I played was that of "Mother Nature" being choked to death by toxic waste! Another time, I was a box of cereal going stale on the shelf at a local supermarket known for charging unreasonably high prices. Then I played the role of the "city official" determined to evict squatters in an abandoned building near Columbia University.

These parts were a far cry from Queen Esther, or Florence Nightingale for that matter, but in my way, I tried to be a modern-day heroine defending what I felt was basic to human survival. I kept up much of this activity

after college, and got a good job writing advertising copy
for J.C. Penney as well. I thought to myself, "I will do this
advertising job for a while, until I can write something
important." I was productive and pleased that my life had
purpose and great potential.

In all this, I was not looking for God—but apparently
God was looking for me.

As I was walking in midtown Manhattan on my lunch
hour, I couldn't help but notice a man who was
conspicuous because of his extremely blond, long hair.
He was wearing a sticker on his shirt, one that I had
been seeing affixed to people's shirts for days. Being a
naturally inquisitive person, and also finding this young
man somewhat attractive, I wanted to know what the
sticker said. My curiosity was mixed with caution—I
was a street smart New Yorker—so I didn't want to ask
him about it directly. If he was some sort of fanatic, I
did not want to get entangled in a discussion that was not
of my choosing.

I decided the best solution would be to find a pretense
for getting close enough to read the sticker myself. All
this happened within seconds, so I stopped him with the
first thing that came to mind: "Excuse me, I was
wondering, would you mind telling me . . . is your hair
really that color, or do you dye it? He smiled, and
assured me that his hair was not dyed. Meanwhile, I was
able to read the words printed on the sticker: "Smile.
God loves you."

Such a statement would not have caught my interest,

except that I had recently read a cover article in *Time* magazine about the California "Jesus People." This guy certainly didn't look like a New Yorker, with his extremely blond hair and what I considered somewhat of a "Beach Boys" look. Instead, he seemed to fit in with the people whose photos I'd seen in the *Time* piece. Who knew, maybe the "Jesus People" were having a convention in New York that week. I could picture the sign at Madison Square Garden: "Welcome, Jesus People." At any rate, I was curious to know if I was talking to "one of them." So I mentioned the article and asked, "Are you one of the 'Jesus People'?"

He told me that he was a "Jesus person," and he then invited me into a nearby coffee shop. It was there that he told me in more detail what believing in Jesus meant to him. This was actually the first time I had ever heard what is called "the gospel." He told me that Jesus was the Messiah, that he came to die for the sins of humanity, that he conquered death—and that by accepting his sacrifice I could have my sins forgiven and live for eternity with my Creator.

Well, I let Larry know I was Jewish and that Jews don't believe in Jesus. I figured there might be an awkward moment, maybe even a mumbled apology, and then we would talk about something else. But Larry continued to talk as if Jesus were still relevant to the discussion. Then he invited me to a church in New Jersey. I explained to him that I had been to the "biggest, most impressive" church Christians had to offer, and I wasn't impressed. He looked puzzled and I explained that I had traveled to Europe and while in Rome I'd visited the Vatican. He smiled and told me that he wasn't inviting me to view an edifice, but to experience a service—actually a concert—in the church. It wasn't until later that I discovered that Larry Norman was a fairly well-known Christian folk-rock singer and that he would be playing guitar and singing at that church.

I went to Larry's concert and was impressed by some of what I saw and heard. The people were young and seemed to have an idealism that was, in some ways, like my own. Of course, they weren't Jewish, so I was certain that what they believed was not for me—still, I respected them.

As for Larry, he and I became friends. I found him kind, creative and contemporary in his outlook, even though he had certain standards of morality that one didn't often come across in the big city. My friendship with Larry, my curiosity and my avid interest in reading were enough to convince me to look into the Bible. That was a life-changing experience.

Now to me, "the Bible" meant the Jewish Bible. I owned a Bible published by the Hebrew Publishing Society (in English) and I knew it was the right Bible for me to use. I began in Genesis.

Once I opened up the Scriptures, it didn't take long to discover the fact that God is holy. That might sound obvious, but I had never really contemplated God's holiness. I could also see that the Bible was not an ordinary book, and that the God of Abraham and Sarah was no ordinary god. I had not been interested in God before because, quite simply, I had a fuzzy idea of who he was.

However, what the Bible revealed about God made me hungry to know more. There was something so wonderful and right about God that I could not help being attracted to Him. However, the discovery of God's holiness had led me to another revelation—I was unholy. My own spiritual need became evident for the first time.

It had never occurred to me that I had "spiritual needs" because I didn't know what that meant. If I would have heard the phrase, I might have thought it meant a lack of meaningful activities, a lack of meaningful relationships or some other social or psychological deficiency. I was not lacking in those areas. Yet I was faced with the fact that a holy and just God created me and had certain expectations of how I should behave and relate to him. I realized that I barely knew God and I felt inadequate to initiate any move to draw closer to him.

Some of what Larry had said to me in that coffee shop began to make sense. God was worthy of my devotion, yet I was not capable of winning his approval. All the good and right things I could do seemed inadequate to bridge the divide between this awesome God and myself. All this added up to spiritual need.

I continued to read the Bible and to discuss these things with the new acquaintances I'd met through Larry. My awareness of this spiritual need and my findings from

the Bible caused me to view the things they said in a
different light; I was no longer merely hearing about
someone else's religion. They were talking about things
that were of deep interest to me—things that I was seeing
in my own Jewish Bible.

I couldn't help but wonder at this point if Jesus might
be who they claimed he was—my Messiah. After all, I
could see that I was incapable of getting any closer to
God on my own. Could Jesus be the bridge, the way into
God's presence? I knew from the Scripture passages I'd
already read that Jesus seemed to fit the description.
The prophet Micah said he would be born in Bethlehem.
I knew that was Jesus' birthplace. Moses pointed to a
prophet greater than himself. Could that be Jesus? King
David described the manner of Jesus' death long before
crucifixion was used. And Isaiah 53—which talked
about an innocent person who would suffer and die for
the sins of others—really clinched it. I had to know.

Within days, I went back to the church where Larry had
sung. I had just been promoted from junior copywriter to
full copywriter at the company where I was employed. I
had the love of my family and friends, a nice place to live
and a promising future. I should have been very happy
that night. But as I sat in the church service, all I could
think of was the fact that I was in the midst of holy things,
and I felt unholy. I knew I didn't belong—not because I
was Jewish or because anyone had passed judgment on me.
I knew I didn't belong because these people had a
relationship with God, and I didn't. I knew that Jesus just

might be the promised Messiah, and I was frightened.

I left the church building and sat out on the front lawn, hoping it would calm my fears. It was a summer night and the air was warm. I knew I had a choice to make as I sat cross-legged and looked up at the stars (something you can't do in the city). There's something about looking at a slice of creation that makes conversation with the Creator very appropriate and natural. I told God that I, too, wanted to have a relationship with him. I found myself tearfully confessing to him right then and there that I believed Jesus was the Messiah. I accepted the fact that he had taken the punishment for my sin, just as the prophet Isaiah had written, "All we like sheep have gone astray; we have turned, every one, one to his own way; and the LORD has laid on him the iniquity of us all" (53:6). I told God that I wanted the forgiveness he offered through Jesus, and that I wanted to live for him. He heard my plea and that night he changed my life forever. He gave me the assurance that his promises in the Bible are true and lasting and not based on wishful thinking. Unlike the rabbi who eight years earlier had told me that, "we can only hope" that there is something beyond this present life, I now had a strong basis for my hope. It was rooted in my Messiah.

As far as I knew, I was the only Jewish believer in Jesus on the face of the earth. Now I had to find a place where I could worship with other people who believed that Jesus was the Messiah. I dismissed what I saw as "establishment churchianity." Instead, I gravitated toward an African-American church. While it wasn't culturally Jewish, at least it was culturally ethnic, and that made me feel more comfortable. In the beginning, I attributed a number of things to Christianity which were simply a part of that particular church's culture. All the women wore hats, so I assumed that just as Jewish men wear *yarmulkas* in synagogue, Christian women wear hats in church!

I didn't expect my family to be overjoyed with my decision, but the priority of God in my life overshadowed whatever fears of rejection I may have had. Still, I wasn't quite prepared for my mother's reaction. "Susan," she said, "it would have been better if you had come to tell me you were on drugs or pregnant." Other family members expressed the gamut of responses—shame, embarrassment, anger, pity and disappointment.

I was completely taken aback by the way my non-Jewish roommates responded. Neither of them had ever used the name of Jesus as anything other than a swear word, until I decided to believe in him. Then they tried to "shake me loose" of what they saw as "archaic superstition." Church and Christianity had been present to some extent in their upbringings, though mostly as a cultural experience. Each felt shocked and disappointed that I, as a Jew, would "regress" to a religion they felt they had outgrown. My Jewish roommate showed no sympathy either. She was sad that I had "gotten religion."

Meanwhile, the reality of God became more and more

sharply focused in my life. After work, I would go to
midtown Manhattan, passing out gospel pamphlets I had
purchased and tell whoever would listen about how Jesus
had changed my life and how he could do the same for
them. I suppose, to some, I had become a "fanatic." Years
later, I remember someone saying to me, "I wish I believed
enough in something to be considered such a "fanatic."

Three months after I had made my decision to believe
in Jesus, something tremendous happened. I was talking
to a Christian couple, and they casually mentioned
something about the other Jewish believers they knew.
"Others?!" I said. "You mean there are actually other
Jewish people who believe the way I do?"

I couldn't wait to meet these other Jewish believers in
Jesus and I was not disappointed; it was like "coming
home." It helped to know people who understood some of
the hardships of being Jewish and believing in Jesus. I
began to understand distinctions between Gentile culture
and Christian theology. I was able to set aside certain
things which had felt a bit strange and alien to me without
setting aside my belief in Y'shua (Jesus). I didn't have to
begin each prayer with phrases like, "Our dear gracious
heavenly Father, we come unto thee in prayer . . ."

As I met more and more Jewish believers, my
understanding of Jesus as the Jewish Messiah also
deepened. I studied the promises God made to our
people, and I began to see how being Jewish gave me even
more reason to trust Jesus. I also came to appreciate that
negative reactions from Jewish friends and family were not

about the specific beliefs I held. They were based on the emotional supposition that it was generally wrong for Jews to believe in Jesus, because he is viewed as the god of the Gentiles—those who have hated and persecuted us.

I wanted to use my cause-oriented zeal as well as my experience in writing and drama to help dispel these misunderstandings. My first idea was to travel in a converted school bus with a few other Jewish believers I had met and proclaim our message across the country. We often discussed such plans, but among the four of us, I think I was the only one who really expected anything to come of it.

Then the opportunity came to move to Northern California to be part of a community of Jews who believed in Jesus and I took the plunge—becoming one of the founders of the Jews for Jesus organization. I used my political drama experience to write original street theater and helped found the New Jerusalem Players, which was the dramatic "arm" of Jews for Jesus. I had opportunities to use my writing skills as well, putting together position papers and press releases that helped make known the message on a national, even international scale, that Jews can believe in Jesus.

I had always wanted to make a difference for the better, to do something meaningful with my life. Moishe Rosen, the actual founder of the modern day Jews for Jesus movement, once told me that I needed to measure how I used my life from a spiritual vantage point. He suggested I put my greatest efforts into "doing those things that would make a difference a hundred years from now." That was good advice.

There are so many worthwhile endeavors in which we can invest our lives, causes that can bring comfort and relief, improvement and a better quality of life to others. But most of these things can only help for a time. They can only address the symptoms, not the source, of life's problems. They don't provide eternal solutions. They don't provide answers for the person with terminal cancer or for the person who is the object of racism and bigotry. They don't bring an end to hunger or war or violence. People need a hope and a future that offer justice and mercy and healing beyond this life, and that is only possible through a personal relationship with Y'shua the Messiah.

Those truths came home to me in a very personal way when, at age 34, I received a breast cancer diagnosis. The oncologist explained that while she didn't want to be discouraging, I needed to know that the tumor was an aggressive one. "So how long do I have?" I asked. She said we can't know such things, and that she had no guarantees to offer—but an aggressive treatment was my best shot at survival. Survival in cancer terms usually means five years. The aggressive treatment she was talking about meant surgery and chemotherapy. And I might add, lots of prayer.

I'd had all kinds of plans. I had envisioned lots of years ahead. Suddenly, I had to take stock of what might be an overwhelming obstacle to my earthly future. One of the hardest things I had to do at that point was tell my family. Whereas I was not looking to shorten my stay on this earth, I honestly believed that my existence would not end here. I had a future and a hope beyond this world. But I knew my family didn't share that hope. Like the rabbi at my father's *shiva*, they were uncertain and unsettled about life beyond the grave. It was no surprise that they took the news very hard. They felt helpless. While I tried to assure them that I would be okay, no matter what the outcome, they took little solace. Yet I believe that my faith made the difference, and I hope that they could see that.

I won't say that the next couple of years were easy. The emotional pain of losing a breast was very real, and the physical discomfort of putting poisonous chemicals into my body had its effect. And there was anxiety over every blood test or X-ray until the negative results came through. Yet I can't think of another time in my life when my relationship with God deepened as much. I can honestly say I experienced the joy of having Y'shua as my personal physician, therapist and friend. His presence can really enable us to transcend our physical circumstances. It did for me. One of Y'shua's followers quoted him as saying, "In the world you will have tribulation; but be of good cheer, I have overcome the world" (John 16:33).

The world's religions can't make that claim. But the gift of salvation, of a forever future with God, is available to Jews and non-Jews alike through Y'shua (Jesus). If you are seeking a personal relationship with God, it really is possible. I'd love to introduce you to Y'shua. There's a prayer included in this booklet that you can pray, or if

you're interested in discussing this further, please send in
the perforated card at the end of the booklet or e-mail me
at sueperlman@aol.com.

*Susan Perlman is one of the founders of Jews for Jesus.
She is the editor of* ISSUES: A Messianic Jewish
Perspective *and has written extensively on the subject of
why Jesus is the promised Messiah. Her articles can be
found through accessing the Jews for Jesus website's
e-library (www.jewsforjesus.org/publications).*

Not Looking for Jesus
The Journey of a Jewish Agnostic

by Stephen Katz

I can't remember where I first heard Bob Dylan's music, but when I did, he immediately became my hero—nearly a god. His lyrics mirrored my worldview. He was a rebel and a free spirit who held nothing back as he confronted people's lies and hypocrisy. I loved that! I wanted to be like him. I taught myself to play guitar. After starting on an old black Stella acoustic that I found in my sister's closet, I got a job in a music store and saved enough money to buy the Gibson that hung in the window. I began to see myself as a sort of rough and tumble guy who could break some rules,

*have some fun and live fast.   I stole harmonicas in almost
every key and got pretty good, pretty fast.   But even though
some petty theft seemed to fit in with my new image, it
added to my inner conflict.   Becoming my own person with
my own set of rules was very important to me.   But, for
better or worse, there were certain things about myself that
were not so easy to change.*

My name is Stephen Katz and I was born September 2,
1956 in Highland Park, Illinois.   I'm the youngest of three
children.   My brother, Richard is five years older than me,
and my sister, Heidi, is four years older.

Our father owned and administrated a nursing home from
the time I was nine, and our mother worked in the office.
Before the nursing home there were other businesses, most
notably, construction.   Dad built several houses and had a
pickup truck with the name "Katz and Son" painted on the
side, though my brother, the firstborn, was just a baby at the
time.   The first half of my childhood was spent in Skokie,
Illinois—a very Jewish suburb of Chicago.   Skokie was
known for being a town with one of the highest concentrations
of Holocaust survivors in America.   Some years after we
moved out in 1965, the American Nazi party caused a big
controversy by conducting a march down Main Street in
Skokie.   The drama was such that it became the basis for a
Hollywood movie.

Our neighborhood was fairly mixed, but it seemed to
me that all my parents' friends were Jewish.   I remember
one non-Jewish family who lived across the alley from us.

Ironically, their name was Rosen—a typically Jewish surname.   But these Rosens were Catholic.   Two of the Rosen boys were about my age and we used to play softball together.   At Christmas time, they always had a big, colorful tree all lit-up in their living room window.   I used to stare at their decorated house from our back door window.   There were so many lights.   Maybe they were compensating for all the undecorated Jewish homes on the block!   I knew that Christmas was the Christian holiday in December, but I really didn't know what it was about.   I used to like to watch Mr. Magoo's animated "Christmas Carol" each year.   I'm sure that Santa and Frosty the Snowman were mixed into my understanding of Christmas, too.

I have other childhood "lights" memories.   Hanukkah was always very magical for me.   My mother would sing the blessings as she lit the candles.   This was one of the only times I can remember hearing her sing.   I loved watching the candles glow.   I would turn all the lights out and watch them to the very end, when each tiny flame would finally disappear in a spiral of thin smoke.   I didn't mind being alone in the dining room while everyone else went about their business, probably watching TV.

My grandmother on my dad's side had come over from Poland, my grandfather from Lithuania.   After my grandfather died, my father always made sure to take care of my grandmother—so she always lived very close to us. Grandma Katz was hit by a car the year I was born, the results being a pin in her hip and a severe, lifelong limp.

She was Orthodox, spoke with a strong Yiddish accent and
kept a kosher home.   Her cooking was very different from
my mother's and I didn't especially like it when I was
young.   But by the time I got into high school I had grown
to love some of her "specialties," like chicken soup with
matzoh balls, sweet and sour cabbage soup and especially
her chopped liver.   At Passover, my brother and I would
always help carry up the heavy boxes of *pesadik* (kosher for
passover) dishes from the storage closet in the basement of
Grandma Katz's apartment building.   During the rest of the
year I remember having to pay attention to which
silverware drawer I used, or what the pattern of the
silverware was, so I could be sure I had either the *fleishik*
(meat) or *milchik* (dairy) utensils.

My grandmother had a picture of Chaim Weizman,
Israel's first president, on her living room wall—I can still
see it in my mind.   I don't remember asking who the man
in the picture was, but I became acquainted with this
important Jewish personality at a fairly young age.   During
grade school, I would walk over to Grandma Katz's house
several times a week for lunch.   She and I would visit
together in what I remember as very special times for the
two of us.   She told me how she hoped that I would one day
go to Brandeis University.   She'd look me in the eyes and
simply tell me that I should go to Brandeis because it was a
"good" school.   Of course, I knew she meant that there
were a lot of Jewish students and Jewish programs there.
Plus, it was a step along the way to meeting the nice Jewish
girl she hoped I would marry.   Grandma Katz stressed that

it was important for me to "marry Jewish," and when I was old enough to date this became a frequent subject of conversation. When my brother married a woman who had converted to Judaism, my grandmother let me know that she was surprised and disappointed. I felt bad for my brother and wondered if she had told him about her feelings.

I always felt that my grandmother and I were bound together in a unique way. I remember her with tremendous respect and affection. She was kind, generous and humble. She didn't have much and never wanted more than what she had. She wore plain dresses and lived in a simple one-bedroom apartment. I remember my father arguing with her when he wanted to buy things that he thought she should have. My father used to talk with his brothers about the fact that their mother would give to any Jewish cause that mailed her an appeal. I guess he thought that she was an "easy mark." I was always impressed by her generosity to these causes because it came from her deep love for the Jewish people. And she passed that love to her children and her children's children.

When I was quite young, a boy named Ra'anan and his father came to stay with us for a while. They were from Israel. I didn't know why they were visiting and I still don't. But in doing family research, I discovered that this kind of hospitality was a common practice of my grandfather in Lithuania. He had been active in a Zionist organization and would often host travelers whose trips were related to "Palestine," as it was called at that time.

When I was nine, our family moved in order to shorten

my father's commute to work. A year or two before, my
father had built a nursing home in his hometown of
Waukegan. The Jewish community there was smaller than
Skokie's, but many of my father's childhood friends still
lived in town. Through them, my parents enjoyed an easy
entrance into the Jewish community and Waukegan's
Conservative synagogue, *Am Echod*.

One of my dad's high school friends lived across the
street from us, and our two families were very close. Their
four kids and my brother Richard, sister Heidi and I were
in the same age range. When their father, Dr. Wool,
wanted to find out if someone was Jewish he would ask,
"Are they an Indian?" as a code for "Jewish" since Jews,
like American Indians, came from tribes. A bunch of us
would be standing in their kitchen and if the conversation
turned to someone he didn't know, Dr. Wool would ask,
"Are they an Indian?" It was pretty funny, but we all knew
what he meant. It was also fun to hear Mrs. Wool tell
stories about my father's teenage antics, such as the time
he was caught driving a car across state lines. He was 13
years old.

Though raised in a moderately observant home, my dad
didn't shape our home that way. We really didn't talk
about God. I didn't know anyone who talked about God,
other than the occasional exclamation, "Oh my God!" or
"God forbid!" When it came to Jesus Christ, my mother
would blurt out the name if she were angry or frustrated.
Other than that, he basically didn't exist.

I never thought much about God, though I did talk to him during one brief period of my childhood.   One of my favorite baseball players on the Chicago White Sox, Carlos May, had blown off part of his thumb in a rifle accident while in the army reserves.   During the *Amidah*, our rabbi used to say that we could silently pray our own prayers instead of following the *siddur* text.   I used to take that opportunity to pray for Carlos May.   I liked praying in my own words for something that mattered to me.   I don't remember how I prayed, but it was probably something simple like "God, please help Carlos May's thumb get better."   He did come back to play baseball, but I didn't think much about my prayers actually being answered.

I did wonder about the size of the universe, especially as I lay on my bed waiting to fall asleep.   Having learned in school that the universe is infinite, I tried to picture it going out in space in a straight line, forever and ever—past planets and stars, going farther and farther—with no end in sight.   My mind couldn't make sense of space that never ended, so then I'd try to picture the universe somehow contained in a vast bubble.   That didn't make sense either because then there would have to be something on the other side of the bubble.   But what could be on the other side if there were no more universe!   Then I'd be back at the idea that the universe never ended, which I couldn't fit into my head.   I often fell asleep with such mind-bending puzzles about the universe running through my thoughts.

Though we weren't religious, we were active in the synagogue. My mom was busy with Hadassah and sisterhood and my dad would join the *minyans* when they needed him to make sure they had enough men (ten are required) for prayer. We always took part in special events and holiday services. Purim carnivals were a lot of fun. One year I dressed as "Super-Mordechai"—the Jewish answer to Superman. My mom made me an outfit of dyed thermal long johns, with a big "M" instead of "S" on the shirt. I probably looked ridiculous, but it was fun. Nevertheless, even at synagogue—in the rabbi's sermons— God didn't seem important. The messages were usually about Jewish causes: Israel, survival of Jewish identity, politics, ethics, Jewish history and tradition. I didn't think about it much, and truthfully I didn't listen all that well as I, like many others, whispered with friends during the sermon.

My grandmother was the one person in our family who seemed sincerely religious. I respected her commitment to tradition and her strict observance of the holidays. Everything she was and did seemed Jewish.

We attended *Am Echod*, a Conservative synagogue, built in 1928. I recall the arches and domes and the smell of mildew in the basement, where our classrooms were. One of my Hebrew school friends used to slap a chain against the decaying walls of the bathroom, causing chunks of plaster to fall out. By the late '60s, the entire building was in disrepair, and plans were made for a new building that would be on our side of town.

I attended Hebrew school after regular school, and I also

went to Sunday school.   One year, due to a scheduling
conflict with the building, we had Sunday school on
Saturdays.   Our teacher, Mrs. Levin, wouldn't let us write
anything because it was Shabbat.   We thought it would be
an easy ride, but it was actually more difficult, since we had
to memorize our lessons and be tested orally.   Mrs. Levin
was a kind old lady who loved Bible stories.   We learned a
lot about Jacob, his sons and the twelve tribes of Israel.

We celebrated the holidays and they created an annual
rhythm in our home, but again, we were not religious.   For
example, on Yom Kippur, going to services on the first
evening and the morning was enough for my dad, and
therefore enough for the rest of us.   We came back for
Grandma Katz in the evening when services were over.

Although sitting through the services wasn't a spiritual
experience for me, on the High Holidays I felt a sense of
excitement over seeing the sanctuary filled to capacity.
Waukegan had the closest Jewish community to the Great
Lakes naval training base, so all the Jewish sailors would come
to our synagogue for those special days.   As a kid I found it
curious to see these men in uniform packing out the building.

The drama of the shofar blasts on Rosh Hashanah and
watching the cantor bowing his face to the ground on Yom
Kippur impressed me.   My dad would fast, resting in his
favorite chair in the den.   I wasn't expected to fast when
I was young, but I remember feeling guilty one year when
my mom cooked me a kosher hot dog for lunch.   I felt
bad for subjecting my dad to the aroma, so I ate it quickly
in the kitchen.

I began to fast after my bar mitzvah, but even then I wasn't very good at it. One year I went to see friends (one of whom was not Jewish) after services. As we walked outside together they offered me some popcorn. I took some, started chewing and then, in a panic, I suddenly remembered that I was supposed to be fasting. I began spitting out popcorn on the ground until nothing was left in my mouth. My friends were pretty amused.

I went to Jack Benny Junior High School, which was just a few blocks down from the synagogue. Mr. Benny (his real name was Benjamin Kubelsky) and his family had been members there. His father, Meyer Kubelsky, was named on a plaque outside our sanctuary, along with many others who had given money to build the synagogue. Mr. Benny had a practice of coming to town every year or two, and the days his limousine pulled up were pretty exciting. All of the students would know he was coming to speak with us during lunchtime, so we kept looking out the windows to spot his arrival. I knew, of course, that he would stop by the synagogue first, since it was just down the street.

I was 12 years old when I had my first experience with anti-Semitism. I was in the lobby of our junior high school. A tall, blond girl yelled at me, "Dirty Jew!" I didn't know what I had done or why she called me that. I was well liked by most kids and had certainly never been the object of hatred. In my confusion, the only response I could think of was to yell back, "Go to hell!" I wasn't particularly proud of my

response. I kept it to myself and didn't talk with my
parents about it. I avoided the girl after that, knowing
that she was my enemy.

At that same time, my good friend Art and I were
attending weekly Shabbat morning services. In our
synagogue, Friday night was the bigger service. The old
men and a few old women would go on Saturday mornings.
But my friend Art and I made an agreement with each
other to go each Saturday morning. We were approaching
our bar mitzvahs and this seemed like a way to step up to
the religious plate. After services, we'd participate in the
kiddush and take a little wine or schnapps with the old
guys. I think they enjoyed our presence. We may have
thought we were getting away with something by having the
alcohol, but mostly we felt good being accepted as "one of
the guys." Going to services like that was kind of fun and
it felt right.

As far as Hebrew school, I worked hard to prepare for
my bar mitzvah. I was a good student, and since I learned
quickly my teacher gave me extra material. Leo Grad, my
teacher, was an older man who had come from Europe.
He had a habit of speaking just inches away from my face.
His breath was strong and a string of saliva seemed to hang
like a bridge between his upper and lower lips whenever
he opened his mouth. Despite these unpleasant
peculiarities his positive influence in my life was very
substantial. He was very warm-hearted and loved Judaism
and the Jewish people. He always greeted me with a smile
and was quick to put his arm around me. Once, when I

began to cry because I didn't know my lesson very well, he treated me kindly and didn't add to the guilt I felt for disappointing him.

I used to practice chanting prayers throughout the day, singing the full *kiddush* and other prayers in the shower. I remember the cantor complimenting me one night after he heard me chant some prayers. I felt proud. So in addition to my *Torah* and *Haftorah* portions, I learned to lead the entire *shacharit* (morning) and *musaf* (additional) services—usually the role of the *chazan* (cantor). I did very well and that was important to me.

Mr. Grad invested much of his time to teaching young people what it means to be Jewish. In tutoring us for our bar mitzvahs he helped us to understand the importance of taking our place in the Jewish community. When one of my friends stopped attending weekly services after his bar mitzvah, I remember Mr. Grad reflecting that some day he would come back, that eventually "all do." I always wondered if that was true, whether even those who give up on Judaism inevitably come back. I wondered if this Jewish kid, who preferred partying to praying, would one day return. And I suppose I wondered how things would play out in my own life.

I was one of the first bar mitzvah boys to have his ceremony in the brand new building. The new synagogue couldn't have been more different from the old. It had a big stained glass window of the Tree of Life behind the *bimah* (platform), and smaller stained glass windows along the side wall of the sanctuary. Between all that color and

the rectangular shape, it was clearly a new, modern day for
the Waukegan Jewish community.   Unfortunately, the
stained glass windows, which were predominantly blue and
green, cast a slightly ghoulish pall over everyone.   We
learned to live with it and enjoyed the new sanctuary.
My bar mitzvah was a big event.   I had been eight years
old when my brother was a bar mitzvah.   My parents hosted
his celebration at my grandparents' house where the kids
danced in the garage to music played on 45 rpm records by
Manny Schwartz the DJ.   By the time my bar mitzvah
rolled around, my parents were able to make the
celebration a bigger affair.   We held it in a big circus tent
in our backyard.

   The actual bar mitzvah service went off without a hitch.
I did well on Friday night and on Saturday morning I led
the congregation through the entire service.   It was a great
feeling to lead all the old guys through the prayers.   Of
course they knew more than I did, but on this day I could
appear to know just as much.

   For a short time after my bar mitzvah I continued going
to Hebrew school, but before long my friends and I were
distracted by other pursuits.   We stopped attending
synagogue and Hebrew school, except for Sunday school,
which was mandatory for the next few years.

   I was involved with BBYO (B'nai B'rith Youth
Organization) throughout high school, serving as vice
president of our local chapter.   BBYO focused on building
Jewish community and identity.   My brother and sister had
been active and it was natural for me to get involved.   I

enjoyed making friends with Jewish kids from around the state. It was more a social experience than a religious one—but of course it was fully Jewish.

During high school, my participation in our synagogue dropped. Mr. Grad would call me once in a while and ask me to do things, like chant from the *megillah* (Book of Esther) at Purim. Despite his kind efforts to involve me, like most of the youth, I continued to drift away.

My neighborhood friends included both Jews and Gentiles. None of us was religious. I remember playing basketball with some Lutheran friends and asking them what the Trinity was, because I was curious. They couldn't answer and I didn't pursue it. They did tell me that the New Testament writers were Matthew, Mark, Luke and John, which I thought was funny and not at all religious sounding. After all, I had friends named Mark and John!

I can't remember any friend ever really telling me about Jesus at any time during grade school, junior high or high school years. During my sophomore year in high school, a Jewish friend and I went to a Christian coffeehouse that had just opened up in town. We knew it was a Christian place, but my friend, a dyed-in-the-wool atheist, and I went for the entertainment value. We figured we would could make fun of the Christians and get some laughs, and in fact we did.

My interests in high school were sports and girls. I didn't know if there was a God and I did not care to know. I guess I was an apathetic agnostic. I wasn't going to bother God, if he existed, and I didn't need him to bother me. I followed my parents' tradition towards a strong but secular Jewish identity. I was in honors classes, played on the soccer and basketball teams and was popular. For the first two or three years things were good.

After a disillusioning experience with the basketball coach during my junior year, I decided not to go out for the team my senior year. That same year my grandmother died. It was my first real experience with death and I didn't know how to respond—especially given my bond with her. I went to a 24-hour restaurant to drink coffee all night and think about life. It didn't make sense anymore. If we all die, what's the point? If everything is temporary, where is the meaning? I certainly didn't see any meaning in making money. My parents and their friends were financially comfortable, but they didn't seem particularly happy.

By my senior year, my interests had shifted from sports to music and marijuana. I was getting high on a fairly regular basis. I tried to observe everything and everyone around me, hoping to find meaning. I began to see that friends who did a lot of partying weren't happy either. Some drank a lot. Some smoked a lot of marijuana or used other drugs, but except for brief highs they didn't seem happy or satisfied. I knew I wasn't. I had no interest in turning on Pink Floyd, turning off the lights and staring, stoned, at the little red light on the stereo! Anyway, parties always seemed to end with scandals and stories of who did what and seemed like another dead end.

No one seemed to care about what they were doing or why. Everyone seemed to be going through the motions without bothering to think. I began declining invitations to hang out with friends. I became arrogant, believing I understood what no one else did. I stared at people with critical eyes, not realizing that I made them uncomfortable, until one day a girl told me so. The truth was, I was pretty unhappy. I couldn't produce any great answers to give my life meaning outside of my own cheerless attempts to take control of life and follow my own conscience.

I can't remember where I first heard Bob Dylan's music, but when I did, he immediately became my hero—nearly a god. His lyrics mirrored my worldview. He was a rebel and a free spirit who held nothing back as he confronted people's lies and hypocrisy. I loved that! I wanted to be like him.

I taught myself to play guitar. After starting on an old black Stella acoustic that I found in my sister's closet, I got a job in a music store and saved enough money to buy the Gibson that hung in the window. I began to see myself as a sort of rough and tumble guy who could break some rules, have some fun and live fast. I stole harmonicas in almost every key and got pretty good, pretty fast. But even though some petty theft seemed to fit in with my new image, it added to my inner conflict. Becoming my own person with my own set of rules was very important to me. But for better or worse, there were certain things about myself that were not so easy to change.

Meanwhile, practicing music for hours and writing songs were welcome outlets from what I cynically deemed the mindless pursuits of my friends and family. As I

withdrew from them, my parents and my best friends began
to worry about me.

I decided I would go to college, with the likelihood of
dropping out before long. That's what Dylan had done. I'd
stay close to campus, soak up musical influences, then try
to "make it" in music. I figured I would change my name
like Dylan had. I was trying to escape my identity as an
upper middle-class kid from the suburbs. I wasn't going to
be bound by my upbringing and training. I would carve
my own path.

So I went off to the University of Illinois at Urbana,
determined to create a new identity for myself. I wanted to
be the rebel, the non-conformist. I wanted recognition for
my music. I played in a few shows in dorms or frat houses,
and imagined all kinds of names for myself, but never
settled on one. As I tried to recreate myself, I figured that
I would uncover the real me, only the real me didn't always
match up with the new image I was trying to project. I
still cared about some of the things I had labeled as
meaningless.

Rhetoric was a required course at the University of
Illinois so I enrolled, never suspecting that it would change
the course of my life. The professor, Dr. Palmer, was Jewish
and he immediately sized me up. One day he passed out a
"Peanuts" cartoon and told us to expound on its meaning.
Rather than take the assignment seriously, I wrote a "stream
of consciousness," piece with no punctuation or order. I just
let my thoughts rip across the page. He gave me an "F"
and confronted my blatantly flippant attitude. He told me

that if I didn't want to be there, I should get the "bleep" out of his class. Though I didn't want to care, I respected him for the way he handled me.

I had always gotten good grades. Now that I was trying to be a nonconformist, I figured I'd refuse to "play the game." According to my new attitude, the "F" and what my professor thought about me shouldn't have mattered, but it did. I still cared what people thought and still measured myself at least in part by the achievement my grades reflected. Even though I had already planned to quit school before I started, I found it hard to accept academic failure. I allowed myself to go into a zoology final exam with a "D," but I aced the test and pulled out a "B" for the class. I couldn't shake who I had always been.

So when Professor Palmer assigned a major research paper that was going to count for about 80 percent of our final grade, I was not happy. About six weeks into the semester, I entered his office with a group of students. We were supposed to give a progress report on our papers. When I told him that I had not yet chosen a topic, he told me to wait while he helped the others. He knew what I was about and he resigned himself to saving me, the "troublemaker," for last.

While I waited for my turn, an idea for the paper popped into my head. It took me by surprise and captured my imagination. I was so excited that I interrupted another student's consultation as I blurted out, "Professor Palmer, I'm going to write my paper on why the Jews at the time of Jesus didn't think he was the Messiah." He was interested.   When he'd finished with the others and just the two of us remained in the room, he told me that he too, had looked into the subject and knew something about it. "Therefore," he said, "I'm going to be more critical of your paper than I will be on the others."   Maybe it was payback, but more likely he really cared about his students and knew I needed a little extra challenge.

But I was already motivated to dig into the topic.   I already had a Bible——I'd stolen a Gideon's Bible from a hotel to help my songwriting. Dylan used so much biblical imagery that I thought I should familiarize myself with it. But now I was really ready to explore and discover.

I began my research by acquainting myself with the Jewish ideas concerning the Messiah.   I knew nothing about the concept, other than a vague notion that the Messiah was supposed to change the world for the better. Now I needed to do hard core research and use historical and biblical sources to determine what the Jewish people in the first century were expecting——and why Jesus didn't fit the portrait. I read what traditional Jewish scholars had to say on the subject——as well as what Christian scholars, secular historians and textual critics had written.

The odd thing was, I don't even know how I knew that Jesus ever claimed to be our Messiah in the first place.   I had never read the New Testament.   There were plenty of Christians on campus, but they weren't *my* friends!   I don't remember ever hearing any Christians talking about Jesus in terms of Jewish expectations.   My only explanation is that God put the idea into my head.

I wanted my research to include interviews as well as written materials and I wanted to hear both sides—so I met with two rabbis and two Christian ministers. It was natural to go to the Hillel rabbi since he was right on campus. I found the other rabbi through the Yellow Pages. For the pastors, I selected one because he was the leader of a big Baptist church I had noticed on campus. The other was a referral from my girlfriend. Her brother was a religious Christian who had told her that if she ever needed some kind of help, she should go see this pastor.

I asked the rabbis questions like, "Why do you think the Jewish people of Jesus' time rejected him?" and "What is the Messiah supposed to do and how will our people recognize him?" The Hillel rabbi invested a lot of time talking about the many different Jewish philosophies and sects that were prevalent at the time of Jesus. I have to admit that much of what he said was over my head and didn't seem particularly relevant, but I appreciated his efforts to help me. I went to the synagogue to see the other rabbi and he responded in a more visceral way. He was a Holocaust survivor from Europe and was quite upset that I would even ask why our people did not believe. "In light of the Holocaust" he said to me, "I find this subject abhorrent! Besides which, I'm not going to do your work for you. You need to read more!" He was obviously agitated, though he did recommend some books. I already had those books in hand from my hours in the library, but I didn't say so since it didn't take much to see that he wasn't interested in talking or in my staying any longer.

I asked the Christian pastors the same sorts of questions. There was an odd kind of symmetry, inasmuch as one of the pastors talked about a lot of things that were over my head and didn't seem relevant, quoting from various Christian theologians like Reinhold Niebuhr and Karl Barth. The other pastor responded on more of a heart level.

Of the four clergy with whom I met, the most engaging was the referral, Pastor Dick Foth. As soon as I walked into his office and we were done with introductions, he asked if my questions were for my paper or for Stephen Katz. I was surprised, but not put off by his directness. I let him know that my questions were actually for my paper *and* for Stephen Katz. In the course of my research, I'd begun to realize that my interest was not merely academic. It seemed to be morphing into part of my personal search for meaning.

Pastor Foth told me stories about a Jewish friend of his, Arthur Katz (no relation to me), who was a Jewish believer in Jesus. He described an interaction between Katz and a rabbi, in which Katz asked the rabbi several questions about various Bible passages. Each time, the rabbi would take down a commentary from his shelf to see what the Jewish sages had to say before answering. Finally, Katz asked the rabbi about a verse penned by the prophet Zechariah, which points to a pierced Messiah coming to earth. When the rabbi went to reach for a commentary, Katz stopped him and asked him about his own opinion regarding the meaning of the text. The rabbi had no answer.

The minister ended our interview with a challenge. "Stephen," he said, "the only way for you to know if Jesus was the Messiah, is to ask him into your life. I can tell you that if you do that, you will know the answer one way or the other. If he is just a myth, your life won't change at all. But if he is who he claimed to be—the Messiah of Israel—then your life will begin to change and you'll know it's true." His challenge made immediate sense to me, but I didn't take him up on it. First of all, I'm naturally cautious and this sounded like a huge, potentially life-changing step. But there was something working on a deeper level. I wasn't the greatest Jewish kid in the world, but I was Jewish enough to know one thing: Jesus wasn't for me; he wasn't for my people. He may be for anybody else, but he's *not* for the Jews.

Nevertheless, halfway through my research I was beginning to lean in the direction that it just might be true—that Jesus might actually be the Messiah.

I hadn't heard anything about Jesus or the Messiah as a kid and now I was facing what seemed to be compelling reasons to believe he might be the one. The entire question of the Messiah was essentially Jewish, yet no one had talked about it as far as I could recall.

In Sunday school we learned the major Bible stories about the patriarchs and the twelve tribes of Israel, but there was absolutely no mention of the Messiah. I don't know if anyone in my synagogue even expected a Messiah. Now, I had entered a new world. I found out that there is a huge amount of biblical material on the subject.

As I continued my research, it seemed that the Jewish scholars dealt with the text of key Messianic prophecies in such a manner so that they couldn't possibly refer to Jesus. They would offer several possible explanations that often struck me as being more about who the Messiah was not than who he was or would be. To me, the Christian explanations of these passages were more reasonable. Being a novice to the text, and reading both sides, I asked myself which explanations made the most sense out of the actual text.

One of these passages was the 53rd chapter of Isaiah. I didn't know much about Jesus, but from what I'd begun reading in the New Testament, it sounded like the events at the end of his life. It certainly didn't sound like Israel, which is what most of the Jewish authors said. "We did not esteem him . . . he was wounded for our transgressions . . . the LORD has laid on him the iniquity of us all." The passage speaks of one who dies for "our" sin and is buried. Yet after this occurs he "sees the labor of his soul" and is satisfied, implying a return to life from the dead. It certainly didn't sound like Israel—my Jewish people—and the pronouns seemed to rule out that theory entirely. The prophet identified himself with the people by using the terms "we" and "us." By contrasting the "we" and "us" with the subject of the entire passage, that subject just *couldn't* be Israel, the whole nation. It *had* to be someone else. I wondered, "Could it be Jesus?" And if it were, what would this mean for me? I wasn't really sure.

As I wrote the paper I didn't disclose my struggle—that I, a Jew, was thinking seriously that Jesus might be the

Messiah. I merely reported the views of the Jewish scholars to answer the question I had posed. I got an "A" on the paper and was relieved to be done with it. Perhaps as an emotional defense, I chose to shelve my unanswered personal questions so I could go on living the lifestyle I was comfortable with and pursue my dream of being a singer/songwriter.

The winter break from school was pivotal. At a New Year's party, I looked around the room at all my friends and could not help thinking that we had all "floated down a river" into college. We had been carried along by the expectations that others had ingrained in us. That night, I decided it was time to implement my plan to take my life into my own hands, to quit school and begin to shape my own future. And so I returned for my second semester, but quit within a month.

It wasn't long, however, before I came face to face with my own limitations and failure to be who I thought I could be. I had written a few songs and sung them in a few small venues, but I was intimidated by the talented artists I saw perform at the larger folk venues in town. I found that I lacked the confidence to really put myself out there and audition for those venues. I became frustrated with myself. I was confronted with my own lack of belief in myself and I questioned my level of talent.

Now out of school, I stayed in Champaign/Urbana, first taking a job in a pizza bar and then later in an industrial bakery that supplied the largest grocery chains in Illinois. I worked alongside a lot of guys who had been working their shift for 20 or more years. Of course, when I told my parents I had quit school they were shocked and very worried. They insisted that I see a psychologist for an evaluation. After a friendly conversation in which he probed my dreams of pursuing music (to see if I was fully in touch with reality), he called my parents to let them know that he had deemed me certifiably sane!

Meanwhile, some three or four months after I'd written my paper and shelved the whole Jesus issue, my girlfriend Laura said, "Guess what? Jesus and I got together last night!" Not exactly sure what she meant, I didn't fight her on it. I figured if that made her happy, fine with me. Laura's parents were Finnish immigrants who had raised her in a devoutly Christian home. At some point in high school she had turned her back on her upbringing. As her father might have put it, she "drank, smoked and acted like the devil." Laura and I had been in school together since the sixth grade, but we didn't start dating until after high school graduation. She thought she'd be "safe from Jesus" by getting together with a Jewish boyfriend. When I started writing my paper on Jesus, I had no idea that she was inwardly panicking. Her fears were based on the fact that she knew that Jesus was true, and that she'd been wrong to turn her back on him. Several months later, in a telephone conversation with her sister, Laura prayed to ask God for forgiveness and to begin following Jesus.

In time, Laura began to read the Bible. Occasionally she would ask me what I thought about various passages. She wasn't trying to manipulate me, but genuinely wanted my help as she tried to understand what she was reading. As I looked at the Bible again for the first time since finishing my paper, the questions my research had raised flooded back into my mind. I recalled the one minister's challenge about how to find out if Jesus truly was the Messiah. I also began to watch Laura change. She had always loved being the center of attention, even if at times it meant being loud and obnoxious. I saw her begin to soften and become more considerate of others. She used to love to party, but now she was uncomfortable with even my quiet use of marijuana. She seemed centered and more purposeful about life. She was different and I noticed. In fact, it seemed she had found some of the meaning and confidence that I had been seeking.

I met a few other Christians as well and saw similar qualities. I began to pray in a personal way that I hadn't done since praying for Carlos May as a kid. "If there is a God, show me. And if Jesus is the Messiah I'm willing to find out."

It may sound silly, but I prayed about something else that had an impact on me. Laura and I had an Irish Setter puppy named Lukas that we loved. One day we lost him. That night a furious, Midwest snowstorm dumped several feet of snow and brought bone chilling winds. Lukas was so young and so small that I was sure he'd never make it. I asked Laura to pray that we find him. Instead of agreeing to pray, she kicked it back to me and said, *"You* pray!" I wasn't experienced at praying, but I cared about the dog so I tried. I supposed this could be a test. If we got our puppy back it could be a sign that God was real and cared about us. A couple of days later we got a phone call from someone who had found Lukas—quite a distance away. He had survived the ice and snow and been found, then returned to us. It made quite an impression on me.

That spring, Laura's brother Joel was the bus driver for a Christian music group called "The Living Sound." They were coming to our hometown of Waukegan, and she invited me to come to a church where they were playing. I agreed to go on two conditions: I wanted to drive separately from her and her family and I did not want to sit with them. I had never set foot in a church other than when I interviewed the pastors for my college paper. I felt threatened and would only do it on my terms, independently from them and free to leave at any time. The song lyrics that I heard sounded bizarre. One bouncy medley they sang went like this: "I'm gonna stay right under the blood. I'm gonna stay right under the blood. I'm gonna stay right under the blood . . . where the devil can't do me no harm."

I had just seen *The Exorcist* and had been scared to my bones! The song sounded really creepy to me. What on earth were they singing about? I had no clue. But the brief talk that the preacher gave made sense. He said that some people there might have problems in their lives that they couldn't fix. Maybe some of those problems seemed as large as mountains. But then he said, "Jesus can move mountains." Surprisingly, that made sense to me. I had a problem that I couldn't fix. Life made no sense to me and

that was depressing.   No matter where I looked I couldn't
find meaning.   Money wasn't the answer.   Partying wasn't
the answer.   Nothing on earth lasted.   Life couldn't be
pointless or it wouldn't be worth living.

By now, I had been praying more often.   I believed in
God, though I never really talked about it.   I felt agitated
and wanted answers.   I was just crying out and those
outcries were some kind of a prayer.

Laura invited me to see her brother's group the next
night, but I declined.   Though I felt a "pull" to go, my
inner "push" was stronger.   Maybe I did see something
different and attractive in Christians.   Maybe Jesus *was*
the Messiah, but still—I was Jewish and it just didn't feel
right to move closer to him.   It seemed like it would mean
moving away from my own people.   But that night, when
Laura and her family were at the concert, I was completely
stirred up inside.   I remember actually pacing in my
parents' family room as thoughts raced through my mind.
"What do I believe?   Was Jesus the Messiah?   Why am I
upset?   What am I going to do?   What's going on?"

A few weeks later, I did go to see Joel's music group
again, this time in Dayton, Ohio.   They did the same
presentation that I had seen before, so I knew that at the
end of the concert they would invite people to come up and
talk with band members—either to receive Jesus into their
life or to talk over personal matters.   I prayed an unusual
prayer.   "God, if you want me to go up there, you have to
get me out of my chair and move my legs."   I felt
completely unable to take such a step on my own.

At the end of the concert, I did walk forward to find Laura's brother. He said, "Hi, Steve. What's happening?" "I don't know, Joel," I responded, "but I want to know Jesus." He sat down with me and, to make sure I knew what I was saying, he opened a Bible to take me through a few verses.

Joel asked me a very important question. "What do you think your family will say about this?" Of course I knew that receiving Jesus wouldn't please my family and that telling them about such a decision could be pretty rough. But something important had occurred. The approval of my family and even my community, which mattered very much to me even when I was trying to be a rebel, had come to matter less than the approval of the God of my ancestors. At the end of May 1975, I took that step of receiving Jesus into my life.

I discovered that Laura had mobilized a lot of people to pray for me to recognize and follow Jesus. In fact, on the night that she prayed with her sister to follow Jesus, her first impulse afterwards was to ask her sister to pray for me. Her sister said something to the effect of, "Laura, don't get your hopes up." But Laura's hopes *were* up and she didn't stop praying and believing that God could get through to me.

On my drive back to Illinois that night I stopped at a gas station to use the rest room. I stood in front of the mirror staring at my reflection. Was I the same or was I different? I looked the same. My hair wasn't blond, my eyes weren't Asian, my skin wasn't black. I was still the

same Jewish kid I had been a couple hours earlier.   But in
some real way that was difficult to understand, I knew I
was different inside.   I felt lighter and more hopeful.
I began reading the Bible voraciously.   I started going to
Dick Foth's church each week.   I was still working at the
factory, and I started telling everyone about the changes in
my life.   Many of my co-workers were African American,
and as I talked with them about Jesus many invited me to
visit their churches.   I was having a great time.   I found
out about a Christian outreach of college students to high
school students and I got involved.   I was the only Jew on
the volunteer staff of 25.

But then there was my family.   What would I say to
them and how would I say it?

I decided to see, without saying anything, if they would
notice the changes in my life.   I had not been very
communicative with them (or anyone) for a couple of years.
I had been so wrapped up in myself, posturing as a cynic.
But now, whenever we spoke by phone I let my parents
know that I loved them.   I hadn't said that in a long time.
We talked like parents and children should talk.   Over the
summer, our relationship began to heal.

That fall, when I went home for my birthday, I told them
about my faith.   I was pretty nervous.   As we sat in the
den, I said, "You remember the paper I wrote about Jesus a
year ago for school?   Well, I've come to believe that he *is*
our Messiah."   The conversation wasn't easy, especially
when my mother started to cry.

Later that night, my father couldn't sleep and I heard him

walk downstairs to the den.   I followed him, knowing how
upset he must be.   As we talked, he wondered out loud how
my friends and I could all go to college with such differing
outcomes.   One studied business, another engineering and I
come home and say I believe in Jesus.   It was a complete
mystery to him, which is understandable.   I don't know if I
could fully have explained how I came to believe.

Meanwhile, my mother thought I had been brainwashed
and that someone had "spoon-fed" Christianity to me.   She
also believed that I wanted to assimilate into Gentile
American society.   The United Nations had just passed a
resolution equating Zionism with racism.   "Stephen," my
mother warned, "there is going to be a new wave of anti-
Semitism in this country and you're just trying to hide."
There was nothing I could say to change her perspective.
Only time could make a difference.

As I continued to work in the factory and grow in my
faith, I began to sense something from my Bible reading.
God is incredibly concerned for the downtrodden in
society—the poor, the orphans, widows, all those who are
hungry, homeless and lost.   The more I read, the more I
sensed that I needed to involve myself in these causes.   I
decided to return to school.   I got my bachelor's and
master's degrees in social work and was employed in the
field of child welfare for ten years.   I worked with children
and teens who were wards of the state of Illinois, usually
after having been abused and neglected.   We cared for
them on many levels and as they reached the age of 21,
prepared them for independent living.

Three weeks after I graduated with my bachelor's degree, I married my girlfriend, Laura. We had a Jewish wedding while expressing our faith in Jesus. It was not easy for my family, but thankfully they did come. My family has demonstrated an ability to put loving relationships above anything that might separate us. While I've seen other Jewish believers lose family relationships because of their faith, this did not happen in my case. Sure, there were many awkward—even tense—moments, but we never lost sight of the love that holds us together. I have been praying for my family to know Jesus as their Messiah for over 25 years, and I believe that God is at work in their lives.

Laura and I now have four children: Hani, Arieh, Talia and Mikaela. Their names are all derivatives from Hebrew. Laura and I spent our second year of marriage living on a kibbutz in Israel, during which time we fell in love with a few names that we decided to use for our own children.

We have raised our children with the knowledge that Jesus is the promised Jewish Messiah, and also with an understanding of what it means to be Jewish believers in him. In our home we celebrate the Jewish holidays and our kids have all had bar and bat mitzvahs as a way of expressing their intent to identify with our people.

After eight or nine years in my profession, I started to get another sense about the work I was doing. I began to recognize that as important as the help we gave to the young people we worked with was, it was also essentially temporary. Remember, much of my search involved a

longing for meaning and for something that would last. I
began to think about the fact that even the good work I was
doing wouldn't last forever. If I helped a teen get a job or
find an apartment or learn to function well in society, none
of those things would matter once his life was over. None
of those things would matter in eternity. Somewhere along
the way I had heard that there are only two things that last:
God's word and people. The Bible says, "The grass withers,
the flower fades, but the word of our God stands forever"
(Isaiah 40:8). It also says, "many of those who sleep in the
dust of the earth shall awake . . . some to everlasting life,
some to shame and everlasting contempt" (Daniel 12:2).

In addition to my growing desire to invest myself in
something lasting was my love for my own people. My
family and I were active in a Messianic Jewish
congregation, and I had always taken opportunities to
speak with Jewish people who were interested in my faith.
So it all came together for me that I should invest all my
time and energy in people and the word of God. I applied
to join the staff of Jews for Jesus. I would strive to reach
my own people with the good news that our Messiah has
come and that his name is Y'shua—Jesus.

I've been serving with Jews for Jesus since 1989. In
that time I've served in Los Angeles, San Francisco and
Washington D.C. I've had the chance to oversee our
traveling music team, write some songs and produce some
albums. I find it incredible that God has allowed me to
use those strands from my past—social work skills and
musical talents—to serve and honor him. Missionary work

is sometimes difficult, monotonous or just mundane. At
times, it's standing on street corners for hours, facing
unpleasant comments and rejection. At other times it
might involve writing reports or sitting in planning
meetings. But in its best moments it's sitting with people,
my own people, one on one—discussing the Bible and
watching God work in their lives. It's praying for people
and seeing hearts and lives change.

Life is filled with little ironies. A few years after I began
following Jesus, Bob Dylan also professed faith in him as the
Messiah. I don't know where he stands now on the issue. I
do know that following Jesus blends two seemingly opposite
strands. True followers of Jesus *are* non-conformists.
Think what you will about Christianity as a dominant culture
in the United States, but the truth is that Jesus' teachings are
far more radical than most people care to think. And for a
Jew, clearly there is a rather painful choice to depart from
the prevailing Jewish notion of who Jesus is. This makes us
non-conformists whether we care to be or not.

At the same time, true followers of Jesus are willing to
conform to ideas, attitudes and, perhaps most important,
hopes which originated in the Jewish Bible, but have been
lost to so many of our people today. I had no idea when I
was trying to recreate my identity that God had a very
different spiritual makeover in store for my life. He knew
I was looking for meaning and something that would last.
He didn't force it on me, but when I began asking leading
questions, he somehow provided the answers that pointed
to Jesus.

I don't know if you believe in Jesus or not.   If you do, please share this booklet with others who might want to hear my story.   Perhaps they will be challenged to take an objective look at Jesus' claims to be our promised Messiah. If you are not sure whether Jesus is who he claimed to be, but genuinely want to know, I'm confident that God will provide answers for you just as he did for me and for so many others.   And if I can have a part in helping with that, I'd be happy to hear from you and to try to answer any questions you might have.

Conclusion

We don't know if you believe in Jesus or not. If you do, please share this book with others who might want to hear these stories. Perhaps they will be challenged to take an objective look at Jesus' claims to be our promised Messiah. If you are not sure whether Jesus is who he claimed to be, but genuinely want to know, we're confident that God will provide answers for you just as he did for Karol, Stephen, Susan, Shlomy and so many others. Below are some statements and Scripture passages that might help you on your journey as you consider whether or not Jesus is the promised Messiah:

God is concerned with every aspect of your life.
"Can a woman forget her nursing child, and not have compassion on the son of her womb? Surely they may forget, yet I will not forget you. See, I have inscribed you on the palms of my hands . . ." (Isaiah 49:15 16a).

You can't truly experience God's love because of sin.
"But your iniquities have separated you from your God; and your sins have hidden His face from you, so that He will not hear" (Isaiah 59:2).

God provided Y'shua (Jesus) to be your sin-bearer and Savior.
"But he was wounded for our transgressions, He was bruised for our iniquities; the chastisement for our peace was upon Him, and by His stripes we are healed" (Isaiah 53:5).

You can receive forgiveness of sins and a personal relationship with God by asking Y'shua to reign in your heart.

". . . if you confess with your mouth the Lord Y'shua and believe in your heart that God has raised Him from the dead, you will be saved. For with the heart one believes unto righteousness, and with the mouth confession is made unto salvation" (Romans 10:9,10).

If you find this to be true, would you consider making the prayer below your own?

"God of Abraham, I know that I have sinned against you and I want to turn from my sins. I believe you provided Y'shua as a once and for all atonement for me. With this prayer, I place my trust in Y'shua as my Savior and my Lord. I thank you for cleansing me of sin, and for giving me peace with you and eternal life through the Messiah's death and resurrection. Please help me be faithful in learning to trust and love you more each day. Amen."

Whether you prayed this prayer or not, please take the time to fill out and mail back the perforated back flap of this book.

If you would like to read other stories of Jews who are for Jesus, check out the Jews for Jesus titles below or go to our web site www.jewsforjesus.org for more information, e-mail jfj@jewsforjesus.org or write to the address on the back cover.

Books:
- *Testimonies of Jews Who Believe in Jesus*, Ruth Rosen, Editor
- *Jewish Doctors Meet the Great Physician*, Ruth Rosen, Editor
- *The Last Jew of Rotterdam*, Ernest Cassutto
- *Between Two Fathers*, Charles Barg, M.D.
- *Bound for the Promised Land*, Haya Benhayim with Menahem Benhayim

Booklets:
- *Drawn to Jesus: The Journey of a Jewish Artist*, David Rothstein
- *Who Ever Heard of a Jewish Missionary?*, Bob Mendelsohn
- *Hineni: Here Am I, But Where Are You?*, Tuvya Zaretsky
- *From Generation to Generation*, Steve and Janie-sue Wertheim

DVDs and Videos:
- *Survivor Stories: Finding Hope from an Unlikely Source*
- *Sam Rotman Concert Pianist: The Music and Testimony of a Jew for Jesus*
- *Forbidden Peace: The Story Behind the Headlines*